Holy Mary of Guadalupe, Ever Virgin

Prose and Poetry of the Mother of God, Our Queen

William Reams
Our Lady of the Holy Spirit Monastery
2625 Highway 212 S.W.
Conyers, GA 30094-4044

Holy Mary of Guadalupe, Ever Virgin
Prose and Poetry of the Mother of God, Our Queen

By Brother William Reams, O.C.S.O.
Our Lady of the Holy Spirit Monastery
Conyers, Georgia

With the permission of
Father Francis Michael Stiteler, Abbot,
given June 29, 2005, the Solemnity of Saints Peter and Paul

Third Printing

Published by
Ann R. Griffin Graphic Design
718 S. Bella Vista Street
Tampa, Florida 33609

International Standard Book Number 0-9669329-1-9

Cover painting by John Gutcher, Tampa, Florida

Holy Mary of Guadalupe, Ever Virgin

Prose and Poetry of the Mother of God, Our Queen

The joy of all is indescribable.
(From the letter of Bishop Juan Zumarraga to Cortes, Christmas Eve, 1531)

To My Earthly Mother
and
My Heavenly Mother
and

To Dom Bernardo Olivera, Abbot General of the Order of Cistercians of the Strict Observance

"A great sign appeared in the sky, a woman clothed with the sun, with the moon under her feet, and on her head a crown of twelve stars."

(Revelation 12,1)

"The great sign that St. John the Apostle saw in the sky, a Woman clothed with the sun, the Liturgy of the Catholic Church not improperly interprets of the most blessed Virgin Mary, the grace of Christ the Redeemer, Mother of all men."

(Pope Paul VI, "Signum Magnum," May 13, 1967, AAS, Year and Vol. 59, n. 7, 28 June 1967)

"...the Immaculate Virgin, preserved free from all guilt of original sin, on the completion of her earthly sojourn, was taken up body and soul into heavenly glory, and exalted by the Lord as Queen of the Universe, that she might be the more fully conformed to her Son, the Lord of Lords and the Conqueror of sin and death."

(Dogmatic Constitution on the Church, ch. 8, n. 59, Second Ecumenical Council of the Vatican)

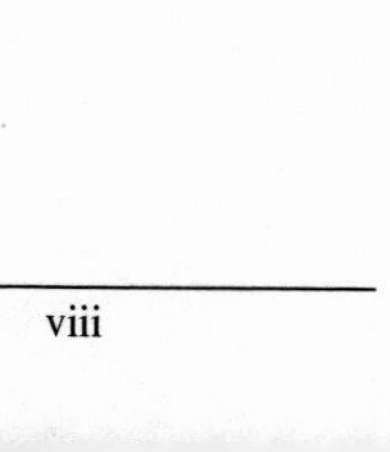

Preface

Our Lady of America, Our Lady of Perfect Love

This book is the fulfillment of a promise.

Many years ago I heard the story of the great Franz Werfel's literary masterpiece, *The Song of Bernadette*. He was a German Jew, a writer who had rebelled against the Nazi's during the Second World War. He was fleeing Germany by car with his wife, enduring great hardships in his effort to escape. They had reached southern France and were near Lourdes. Someone told him he might find lodging there for the night. Though not a Catholic, he had heard the story of Lourdes and made a vow to the Virgin Mary that if she would deliver him he would sing *The Song of Bernadette* in a book.

She delivered him, and he kept his vow.

In the summer of 1969 I was fresh out of Our Lady of Peace Psychiatric Hospital in Louisville, Kentucky. I had spent three months there recovering from what the doctor called "a nervous breakdown," as it turned out, the first of several. I was walking in our large monastic church, trying to pray, considerably unsettled about the future. I thought of Franz Werfel, and then of a picture of Our Lady of Guadalupe of Mexico that I had seen on the Abbot's desk. In a kind of hopeful desperation I prayed, "Holy Mary of Guadalupe, if you'll keep me on the right track, I'll write a book about you."

Perhaps it was a kind of "holy presumption," and it certainly wasn't as gracefully put as Franz Werfel had put it – but I meant it every bit as much as he did. By "the right track" I meant the way of full fidelity to her Son Jesus Christ in my Cistercian vocation.

Now if anybody thinks it's easy to write a decent book about the Queen of the Universe, he or she should think again. The Cistercian humanist, spiritual director, and author of the beautiful *This Tremendous Lover*, Dom Eugene Boylan, compiled 600 pages of notes for his book on Mary, but he never wrote it.

And yet love does make it easy. Dom Boylan was an excellent theologian, and his idea of the Church as the "mystical womb" of Mary still lives in my memory. Mary, the "woman clothed with the sun" of the Book of Revelation, with "the moon under her feet, and on her head a crown of twelve stars," crying out in the agony of childbirth (Revelation 12, 1-2) – this is Our Lady of the "genesis" of Father Pierre Teilhard de Chardin, SJ, Our Lady of Love, bringing Christ to birth in us.

I had heard of Guadalupe before noticing this picture on the Abbot's desk. I had seen representations of the miraculous image several times, usually rather small and rather poor reproductions. But this picture was larger and quite accurately reproduced. What a world of difference! It was art. It was prayer. The face was dark and chastely, strongly feminine. The young girl's sway over one's heart and mind issued from the simple power, the absolute integrity of her personality. Her lowered eyes were not so much downcast as focused on a Center of the universe that lay in her Heart. I had surrendered mine to this wonderful Lady many years before, when as a boy of about 13, I looked up at her statue standing on the top of the chest of drawers in my little bedroom – and loved her. From that moment it had belonged to the most blessed and glorious Ever Virgin Mary.

It was the same "most resplendent Virgin," who on her first appearance to the "little son" she chose out of all the Americas, the very human Juan Diego, had told him she was Holy Mary of Guadalupe, the Ever Virgin Mother of God. The substance of her message, "as to someone greatly esteemed," was that she loved him, and all his fellows who love her in return, who hope in her and ask for her help. She left him and all the world a picture of herself, which today still hangs in her temple there in the Valley of Mexico, ringed by spectacular snow-capped mountains.

Indeed, when Sir Walter Raleigh put his cloak at the service of Elizabeth, Queen of England, it had already been half a century since this early American noble, Juan Diego, had surrendered his to the First Lady of the Cosmos, Mary, Queen of the Heavens. It is over 450 years ago now that the Blessed Virgin appeared to this Mexican man, transforming his *tilma* or cloak into a living demonstration for her poor victimized people that the moon is really only made of stone and that God has put it along with all other things under her feet.

Truly, in "Santa Maria de Guadalupe" we have been given and we have found someone most dear and infinitely more than an equal to serve and to live for, someone from whom alone we could have learned to adore with love the tiny Cross she wears at her neck, the God in her Heart.

When Mexicans march behind the image of the Virgin of Guadalupe, it is the whole world that is moving forward. The story of Tepeyac is the epic story of the Church. From the Island of Patmos to Guadalupe and from Guadalupe to the present, "the positive essence," fulfillment, even the survival of civilization, have always meant "a woman clothed with the sun." The very energy of our old earth, source still of the planetary progress of the modern world, is both awakened and sustained by her. For her purity is the power that unifies all of it.

As the Bride of God, Mary is the Hostess in His house. Her hospitality is for all. Our docility, our willingness, our readiness to accept, nay, our very acceptance of her invitation, let these be the song we sing in our heart with the Mexicans of Juan Diego's *tilma*: "Before it forever let me fix my abode."

This is a book about the wonder of Guadalupe. Yet it is not a book merely about some phenomenon, but about some*one*. I take the beautiful story of Guadalupe in Mexico in the sixteenth century as my starting point, but I do not stop with it. For the Virgin of Guadalupe is the Virgin of Revelation, of the Catholic Faith, of Dogma. At Fatima she said, "I am the Lady of the Rosary." At Lourdes she said, "I am the Immaculate Conception." But first of all she had said at Guadalupe, in all simplicity going straight to her basic title, "I am the ever Virgin Mary, Mother of the True God."

This book is about the essence of the Guadalupan phenomenon, and that essence is Mary, the Mother of Jesus Christ. It is about the Virgin, the Mother and the Queen.

But most of all it is about the Queen. The Queenship of Mary has always been held in faith by the Catholic Church, but it was only at the Second Vatican Council in the latter half of the twentieth century that it was constituted a dogma.

I wish to proclaim that dogma. I wish to serve this Queen. I wish to be the apostle of her Universal Queenship: "universorum Regina."

For, Mary, you are the refuge, the defense, the inspiration and the energy, not merely of the Western Hemisphere, but of Western Civilization, and under Christ even the culture of the species, the educator and protrectress of the globe. O Queen of All Things, you are somehow God's very hope for the universe. Yes, the love, the compassion, the help of Holy Mary are indeed for absolutely *all*.

"Hail, O Virgin of Guadalupe! ... while you are recognized as Queen and as Mother, America and Mexico will have been saved," [1] and all the world. You are the glory of the true Jerusalem, the joy of the new Israel, the honor of our people (Judith 15,9) They who reflect your brightness will have eternal life. (Sirach 24,31)

"The last enemy to be overcome will be death ... that God may be all in all." (1 Corinthians 15, 26 and 28) For this reason, may your mercy, Lady, your loving mercy, always remain with us, for we have placed our confidence in you.

[1] Pope Pius XII, Radio Message to the International Convocation at Mexico, October 12, 1945, quoted in The Dark Virgin, Donald Demarest and Coley Taylor, Coley Taylor, Inc., Publisher.

Like Jeremiah, Juan Diego protested, "Ah, Lady, I'm a child!" But the answer is always the same: "To whomever I shall send you, you shall go." (Jeremiah 1,7)

"It is important ... weary as you are."

O my Lady Mary, since it is truly your wish, "Not one thing will I omit to do. Nor do I mind the trouble ... It was only that perhaps I would not be heard with favor, or if I were heard, that I might not be believed." [2] Patroness of Mexico, Latin America, and the Philippines, Empress of both America's, Queen and Mother of All, Virgin of Guadalupe, "I will go do your will."

Smile on me. Help me. Be with me. Let me write nothing but what your Holy Spirit puts into my heart, but let me never be afraid to write the *whole* of that.

"O Immaculate Virgin, Mother of the true God, and Mother of the Church! ... Mother of mercy, Teacher of hidden and silent sacrifice ... We wish to be entirely yours and to walk with you along the way of complete faithfulness to Jesus Christ in His Church: hold us always with your loving hand." [3]

Most holy Mary, here is your book. I know that just as you delivered Franz Werfel from imprisonment and death, so you will deliver me from all infidelity.

And now, most beautiful Lady, now I begin.

[2] "Historia de la Aparicion de Nuestra Señora de Guadalupe," in ...Hvei tlamahvicoltica...(published by Luis Lasso de la Vega, 1649, translated into Spanish by Primo Feliciano Velazquez), Mexico, Carreño e hijo, 1926. Translated from the Spanish by the author.

[3] Pope John Paul II, Prayer to the Virgin of Guadalupe, Mexico, January, 1979.

Holy Mary of Guadalupe, Ever Virgin:
Prose and Poetry of the Mother of God, Our Queen

Introduction

A Rose Named Holy Mary

It is the summer of 1970. I am in a Pan American jet 29,000 feet over Mexico. We start coming down for Merida. The blue above and below is wonderfully beautiful. Out of my window to the left are silver white clouds, below them the limestone Yucatan Peninsula. The land becomes more distinct. Small villages appear, and a town, several towns connected by straight roads, more villages and larger towns with Merida just a few minutes away – churches, smoke in a field, power lines. At the Merida airport the Mexican kids have a ball talking, laughing, gesticulating about all the passengers as we enter the terminal. I laugh too. Customs takes half an hour. Then we're back in the air.

We come into Mexico City toward dusk. Big, big town. We circle the lovely evening lights of the sprawling city in a leisurely approach. It is so alive and yet so peaceful. As I contemplate the sparkling charm through the window I feel very happy. I have come for the love of a Lady.

It is sprinkling as we land. Courteous, smiling uniformed airport attendants meet us with umbrellas as we disembark. I decline the offer with a happy smile. There are perhaps more ladies than umbrellas.

I am to spend four months with the Marist Fathers gathering material for my book. The Vice-Provincial meets me at the terminal with a sign held to his chest with my name on it. He is very courteous and drives me to the parish where I will stay. At the rectory of the Parish of Our Lady Queen of Peace I am introduced to Father Manuel Jimenez who has graciously offered me hospitality. Father Jimenez introduces me to two charming women, the Misses Estella and Maria Enriquez, who are helping him with his office work, and after dictating one more letter takes me up to my room, with which I am delighted.

The next day we visit the shrine, the Basilica of Our Lady of Guadalupe. It is an overwhelming experience for me. The beauty, the peace, the deep, deep joy – and the serenity of the image of Mary looking down in prayer on all her poor children. It is too much. Father Jimenez says quietly, "It's okay," as I kneel there beside the altar, and my tears and soft sobbing begin to abate.

We pray for the Peruvians, who are suffering from a terrible earthquake in which 100,000 people have been killed, whole villages destroyed. And we pray for the whole world.

Having come with the intention of gathering facts, I soon find myself gathering poetry. I will leave Mexico four months later with very few more "facts" than the few with which I had come. But far more precious than a world of facts to me will be the memory of this Lady and the spirit of her people.

It turns out that Father Jimenez loves *The Hymn of the Universe* and thinks that *Seeds of Contemplation* are beautiful. I am glad to find a lover of two of my favorite authors. But I am to find that Mexico has some beautiful things of its own, like the melodies the Carmelite nuns sing over by the Basilica, and the work of the Benedictine monks at Cuernavaca.

I find that there are no screens on the windows in Mexico, at least on most or many of them. Through them you can look out and *see* – the blessed Sacrament of the Universe.

There are mosquitoes, and the fumes in the streets are sometimes rather strong, but the rain always purifies the air, and then the air is very, very good.

Father Jimenez drives me past Chapultepec Park, which goes on and on for miles, and though we don't stop, we see the bison at the zoo, almost the emblem of America's classic past.

How I would like to visit the Museum of Natural History, and Quahutitlan where Juan Diego lived, and the Jesuit Fathers' great historian of Mexico, Father Daniel Olmedo.

But perhaps after those to Juan Diego and Bishop Zumarraga, the most impressive monument, not in size or physical grandeur, but by the resonances of universality that it evokes, is that to Columbus, surrounded by the four Franciscans said to have assisted him in obtaining the royal support.

Yes, Mexico, where inside over the barbershop door hangs a picture of Holy Mary of Guadalupe.

It rains almost every day during the summer in Mexico, south on the high plateau. But some mornings the sun comes out, and then the clouds shine like brilliant white silver, and the blue of the stratosphere is deep and clear, and you can see forever – and all the best of American culture stands massive and solid before the sky in an unambiguous contemporary church.

From the parish house you can hear the singing of the young people at their Mass:

> "Cristo, ten pieda-a-ad, ten piedad de noso-tros.
> Cristo, ten pieda-a-ad, ten piedad de noso-tros."

They really are people, and music is the same everywhere. In strictest truth it is song and melody that are at the basis of sidereal harmony, the music of the spheres, of the biosphere and the noosphere. Where there is the vitality of a great hope, there proportionately to our faith we will discover an unspeakable love.

The concrete horizon outlined against the white clouds of the afternoon sky by the rooftop culture of a big city seems to somehow signify the prelude to, even the beginning of, a new universe. That's what makes the endless blue behind those clouds so wonderful to look at and to love.

Every cloud has a silver lining. This is especially true of the clouds over Mexico, where the rain every afternoon during the summer purifies the city air, divinising our earthly environment. Beyond the clouds the stratosphere is blue, and beyond the building tops, with their TV antennas and washing hung out, that must not be too different from those of New York or many another metropolis, a Lady in rose and turquoise, her hands folded in prayer, her recollected love centering the universe, keeps continual open house in a residence frequented for the most part by the very best families of the area, her chosen Anahuac people.

Here comes the rain.

The International Soccer Games are in progress. Mexico beat Belgium the other day 1-0, and it seemed as if half the automobile horns in the city were honking out their three beep "Me-xi-co, Me-xi-co." But today Mexico lost to Italy, and Mexico is sad. A few horns are still beeping though, even now in the rain. They must be the ones with an eye toward the future.

Meanwhile, up out of the concrete between and along-side the buildings, trees grow in the city, because of this refreshing rain that alternates with the bright sunshine.

Where in all the world are the skies so beautiful in the evening, unless it be at sunset in Florida, or at dusk southeast of Atlanta? And where in all the world does the thunder sound so lazy or the raindrops strike so indifferently against the panes? Or the lightning of God's grace electrify the depths within a man!

The mornings of the enigmatic days are bright with hope, till the clouds begin to weep. But just when the tears seem hateful, suddenly in the silence they have almost stopped, and there is color in the air.

The evening will be lovely.

And someone who wears twelve stars, quietly, in a plain veil over her black hair, will love the city and the land to sleep from her Basilica over there in Villa Gustavo Madero, which she occupies through the centuries, till all her children are born.

O Holy Mary! It is you who are bringing us to birth. And yet we suffer too. Because we aspire, because we love and at the same time don't know how and want to know how, don't know where to bestow our souls, the wondrous uniqueness of our personalities, the dazzling transcendence that is a gift so incomprehensible it mystifies us – we weep. A mystery hidden deep within us, the Gift itself, impels us. We want to give. We want to give the Gift. We want to give our very being, because even the poorest of us realizes confusedly that he comes of a noble lineage which reaches up from the depths of the universe and that he is not worthless – that Someone exists, Someone lives, Someone waits, for whom the stars reach out.

We suffer, and you give us Jesus, Jesus in the Eucharist, the Gift that you give the Church to lay before the Father through the ministry of her priests that the whole world may thus find expression of the longing that is pent up within it, that this poor, blind world, so radically unintelligible to itself, this world we love, may somehow – even despite its fearful but necessary groping which so often issue only in tragedy and that their best often only in tears – realize that it does itself love, and that it may in fact really love.

Everyone must be told: "Peace! It is I. Do not be afraid." We must communicate the whole way this transcendent message of the early morning of the Resurrection, sparkling with clarity: humility, confidence, courage.

Virgin of Guadalupe, let me sing to you. Some say you are Indian, an Aztec Princess. Some say you are a Mestizo Maiden. To me you are just simply human, our Virgin Mother. Other people have virtue. I have you, who are wholly the virtue of Love.

The language of faith: Mary is sufficient, "the grace of Christ the Redeemer," more beautiful than the glist'ning snow, soft and silent, the true balm, Heaven's Key and our hearts'.

If the moving of mountains is irrelevant, the faith is living. It is of man's nature to seek, and to seek so as to find, the sign, *signum magnum*, the *great* sign, "a woman clothed with the sun." The woman is the Virgin. The dragon is the evil one. Michael, "who is like God," is what we must become, the champion of Mary.

Give us faith, Lady, to see our tiny Cross as the jewel, the brooch at your neck adorning your beautiful and sacred person. Channel the expression of our thought. Rule us from within. Live in our minds. Make us love one another as Christ has loved us. Make us work. Teach us to *be*, and we will be one.

It seems that war came to Mexico with the Toltecs in the seventh century and barbarism with the Chichimecs in the twelfth. But among the later Aztecs there was a poor man who needed the Mother of God. You came to him, Mary, and brought civilization to all of us. You will purify, preserve and save it. You will teach us to build a new culture. You will provide us with the energy and the inspiration to serve, and you will make us love it. There is everything to do.

O Mary, you found us sick with bewilderment, and granted our imploring eyes life, hope and the gift of your love. You are truly the divine Lady who enliven and sanctify, fructify and bless all things – under Christ, the cosmic hope of mankind.

His Apostles came first, then His martyrs, then the Fathers of the Church and the monks. After the monks came the knights, and after the knights, who formed a great part of them, the Crusaders. Now with the Conquistadors, Juan de Zumarraga, Bishop-elect, was bringing with him in his own person the faith of Christ to a New World on the ship bound from Spain to Mexico. It was the year 1528. Mexico was "New Spain," and he was the "Protector of the Indians."

Lightly flaming clouds drifting in the evening sky over a city of eight million, as I write, are they not a part of this mystical faith, this transcendent love, and a sign of a barely perceptible but irresistible progress, the universe moving toward Someone? Something has been carried over from the old aboriginal inheritance – "at least the flowers, at least the songs" – something infinitely precious has been carried over and born anew.

People: the cosmos is made of people. There was the day the Basilica of Our Lady of Guadalupe was packed full with the annual pilgrimage from Querétaro. Eight thousand people had walked all the way. It was the Solemnity of Saints Peter and Paul, and I was in the midst of it all. O Blessed Communion! The Gift of Universal Communion.

During my four months stay I go on to have many adventures in the City of Mexico. There is the time I walk all over town looking for a bathrobe. My little Spanish vocabulary book says, "bathrobe – bata de baño." So I walk into one establishment after another with my routine and barbarous question, "¿Tengas ustedes bata de baño?" At one place, after I deliver my query, the group of ladies who are sewing gather up their work and scurry out of the room, and the man points through an open door. They think I am asking to use their bathroom. I explain as best I can, apologize, and *vamoose*. After I have covered nearly half the city, I find myself more exhausted than I ever was before in my whole life, and two blocks from the parish where I am staying I break down and hail a taxi in order to make it back.

Another time I come down in bed with some kind of summer flu. Sister Patricia, a young nun who serves the rectory, brings me a big glass of grapefruit juice, which only whets my thirst. At the next meal I'm able to get to, I blurt out that I could drink of gallon of it. Father Jimenez, very evidently irked, answers in Spanish, "We don't have a gallon."

I try to talk to some of the parish children in my stumbling Spanish. I tell a group of them the story of Guadalupe as best I can. The littlest ones laugh and giggle at my foreignness and my comical Spanish. But one pretty little girl with a flower in her hair, somewhat older than the rest, becomes very reflective, and I feel that I have communicated more than I have understood.

Soon after this it is time for me to leave Mexico. I leave as I came, with tears. For I leave behind me my Sweetheart.

Will I ever be able to return?

I don't know.

But whether I do or not, I retain before the eye of my heart an image of its exquisite mystery, a thoughtful little girl standing there in the patio of Queen of Peace Parish, a pretty little girl with a lovely flower in her hair, a rose I wish I could name

Santa Maria de Guadalupe.

Part One

Prose

Chapter One

Preparing the Way

Mexico

Let us begin the story of Holy Mary of Guadalupe about 20,000 years ago, when via the Bering Strait and perhaps by other ways man first reached America. Five thousand years later he was in what is now the western United States, and in another five thousand years in the Valley of Mexico. A couple of thousand years more, and he had reached Tierra del Fuego off the southern tip of South America. The whole Western Hemisphere was now at least sparsely covered by humanity.

But let us return immediately to that "Valley of Mexico," a little north of the rain forest of Guatemala where the great Mayan culture would flourish. The Valley of Mexico is a circular basin at the southern end of Mexico's high central plateau. It is extremely fertile. Here a large center of trade and culture was to develop in the famous Teotihuacan, long closely related to the great Mayan center of Kaminaljuyu, though never rivaling the very greatest of the Mayan centers. By about 600 AD it seems to have had a population of as many as 100,000 people.

A century later new warrior groups called the Toltecs, who took their name from the mountain pass called Tollan, entered the Valley of Mexico from the north. They conquered Teotihuacan but preserved something of its culture. Close on their heels came the Chichimecs, who – says the Spanish Franciscan, "Motolinia," Fray Toribio de Paredes, who wrote from 1535 to 1540 – "were a barbarous people and lived like savages." Still, even they left something of the former culture for the eighth century Acolhua, who came from the east and were a cultured people themselves. "They tilled and cultivated the land, began to erect homes and to organize towns...to write and compose memoirs..." These "people of Colhua" settled first on the eastern shore of the Lake of Mexico. Then they moved to the south of the lake, where they established their domain, "Colhuacan," where the principal chief lived. To the north at the western edge of the lake "there were then swamps and marshes, barring a small area which was dry land and resembled a small island." Here the Acolhua built a few straw houses. It was the beginning of what was to become "the City of Mexico."

For the Mexica came next – three centuries later, again "by way of the pass called Tollan." They were less civilized than the Acolhua and at first settled to the west a little more than four miles from those "few straw houses" of the Acolhua. Then they went "to Chapultepec, where an excellent fountain rises,"[4] and from there they populated a city.

Then about 1300 AD, in the area of that "small island" among the swamps and marshes of western Lake Tetzcoco, the Mexican Aztecs founded their own city and

[4] History of the Indians of New Spain, Fray Toribio de Benavente Paredes, Academy of American Franciscan History.

named it Tenochtitlan after their leader. At its beginning this city of the Tenocha Aztecs probably numbered a thousand or two.

By the beginning of the sixteenth century its population seems to have been in the hundreds of thousands, and the Mexicans or Aztecs had extended their hold by both trade and war over most of central and southern Mexico and south to what is now Nicaragua. They called themselves *Colhua*-Mexica, wishing to claim some relation to Colhuacan with its continuation of Toltec-Teotihuacan culture.

But Christopher Columbus first learned of them from the islanders of the West Indies.

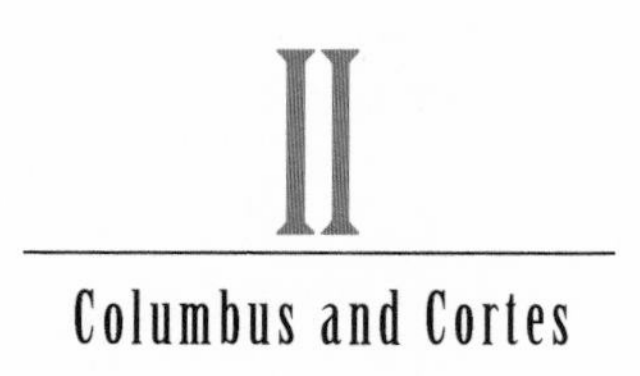

Columbus and Cortes

About 1484, Columbus had been disappointed by a Portuguese refusal. He had left Lisbon for Spain and been befriended by the Franciscan friars at the Monastery of La Rabida near Palos. It seems that it was probably by means of a letter of introduction to the Franciscan confessor to Queen Isabella, given him by one of these friars, that he managed admittance to the court. But the Spanish were occupied with the Moors and referred his plan to a commission. He left for France, where his brother had already gone to try the French court. While he was on his way a messenger reached him: Spain would sponsor him.

Commanding the little flagship *Santa Maria*, Columbus was accompanied on the smaller *Pinta* and *Niña* by commanders Martin and Vincente Pinzon. He spent long hours in prayer on the ship. One day after many at sea he called across the water to Martin. Should they keep going? "Adelante! Adelante!" came the famous reply. It was in the evening air that they thrilled to the lookout's cry of "Land!" Columbus named the island San Salvador and discovered Hispaniola east of Cuba, where his brother Bartholomew would four years later found the Spanish colony of Santo Domingo.

It seems that it was at Santo Domingo that some years after that Hernan Cortes, who probably first studied law for some time in Spain and then decided to come to America to settle, turned soldier. After moving to Cuba from Santo Domingo in 1519, he was chosen by the governor to lead a small expedition into the mainland of Mexico.

In 1511 a Spanish ship had been wrecked off the coast of Yucatan and most of the survivors sacrificed by the Maya. In 1517 Hernando de Cordoba had sailed along the east coast of Mexico, engaged in an unprofitable battle with some of the natives and returned to Cuba with an insignificant sampling of gold. In 1518 Juan Grijalva had sailed a little farther north along the coast and returned to Cuba.

In 1519 Cortes and his little army landed at the island of San Juan de Ulua, and then founded Vera Cruz on the coast. Sending one of his ships to report directly to the Spanish Emperor, he burned the rest of them to prevent any possibility of retreat and to add the crews to his army. The resistance of the coast towns was relatively light, and after awhile he and his five or six hundred men and a few horses were in the midst of a treck through the eastern mountains to the inland center of the country.

Moctezuma II, the Aztec ruler, had not wanted to receive him, but peacefully or otherwise, Cortes was coming. In the end, his insistence that his monarch required communication with the Indian monarch prevailed, and Moctezuma received him in Tenochtitlan.

Meanwhile, the governor of Cuba, suspicious of his loyalty, had sent another army to relieve Cortes of command. Cortes, considering himself in the service of the

Spanish Emperor, left a small body of men in the Indian capital and proceeded to the coast to win over the opposing army.

History records it as "the sad night" when Cortes returned with his bolstered force to learn that the Aztecs had attacked and almost completely slaughtered the small band who had remained. The main body only retreated from the scene at the cost of very serious losses, and repaired eastward to recuperate and prepare for a tough siege.

It was only two years later in 1521 that, assisted by great numbers of the neighboring tribes who were willing enough to support the Spanish in the termination of the cruel Aztec domination, the force was ready. The price of communication proved high. The Spanish took the city, but only with a terrible struggle. The last resistance came at Tlaltelolco, and Cuauhtemoc, a second Indian Emperor since Moctezuma, was captured fleeing with his family over the lake in a canoe.

The monument at Tlaltelolco today reads, "It was neither conquest nor defeat, but the painful birth of a people."

Fray Bartolomé de Olmedo

Beginning with Columbus' second journey in 1493, probably every expedition to the New World had carried missionaries. Cortes' expedition carried the Mercedarian Monk, Father Bartolomé de Olmedo, along with two Franciscans, Fray Diego de Altamirano and Fray Pedro Melgarejo de Urrea.

Father Olmedo was an excellent theologian and a man of good sense. Cortes was zealously religious, but Father Olmedo had to tell him more than once to moderate his zeal and use more order and prudence. Upon arrival at Ulua he had simply explained to the natives that they should not worship their idols and worked hard to show them the horror of human sacrifice and to persuade them to give it up. He also explained the meaning of the Cross. That was all, but it had established contact.

In another place, obliging Cortes to act with more prudence, he would not allow a Cross to be raised. "It seems to me it's not yet time to let them have a Cross in this village. They're bold and fearless and vassals of Moctezuma. They might burn it or commit some sacrilege. What they've been told will do them till they have a better knowledge of our Holy Faith." [5]

[5] History of the Conquest of New Spain, Bernal Diaz del Castillo, quoted in The Spiritual Conquest of Mexico, Robert Ricard, University of California Press.

In Tlaxcala he advised Cortes to leave the people alone until they were more seriously grounded in Christian doctrine. "It's unjust for us to convert them by force....Our warnings are enough." In Cholula also he would not allow the removal of the idols. As Moctezuma did not yet seem disposed to allow it, he opposed the construction of a church at Tenochtitlan. Nor was his ardor extinguished by "la noche triste." He baptized the old *cacique* of Tlaxcala and the young lord of Tetzcoco and offered Mass daily until the wine ran out.

He might not have been the first Catholic priest to see the country of Mexico, but he was the great forerunner of the Church there and its first apostle. When he died toward the end of 1524 the mourning was universal. Cortes wrote that he was a holy man, and the whole city of Mexico wept for him.

Yet how delicate, how fragile was this first influence. How it cried out to be completed by the other giants who one by one, two by two, would struggle their lonely way into the heart, into the consciousness, into the culture of this desert, and into the lives of its people, whom they would serve and love and weep with till their death.

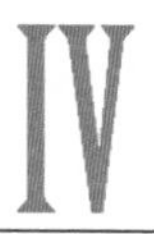

Fray Pedro de Gante

Father Olmedo was the first apostle, but it was the Franciscans who would evangelize Mexico. The beginning of their work may be properly dated from 1523, the year before Father Olmedo died. That was the year Bother Pedro de Gante came.

Born about 1480, probably at Ayghem-Saint-Pierre near Ghent, a Flemish city today included in Belgium, Pedro de Mura, a cosmopolite familiar with many European centers, was a relative of King Charles of Spain. In 1521, when the report that Cuauhtemoc had surrendered to Cortes and had been taken prisoner reached the court, he resolved to become a missionary.

He became a Franciscan brother, took the name of Peter of Ghent, and obtained permission to come to Mexico. Two other Flemish Franciscans, Father Johann van den Auwera and Father Johann Dekkers, known in the Spanish documents as Fray Juan de Aora and Fray Juan de Tecto, both of whom would relatively soon die of hardships on the way to Honduras with Cortes, accompanied him.

On August 30, 1523, when Fray Pedro de Gante was about 40 years old, the three of them landed at Vera Cruz.

They had to walk hundreds of miles, over mountains and through valleys, to Tenochtitlan, now the "City of Mexico" or simply "Mexico," and arrived while thousands of Indians were re-building it. They retired to Tetzcoco not far from the city, where all was quiet, and began studying the Indian languages. Soon they were able to understand them well enough to begin their work.

For 40 years, till his death in 1572, without ever returning to Europe, Fray Pedro de Gante would remain in Mexico. He was to teach generations of Indians the Christian religion at the same time as he taught them to read and write, to paint and sculpture and to work. The very year he came he founded the great school of San Francisco at Tetzcoco, America's first school, which was to have as many as a thousand pupils.

He began technical schools, introducing instruction in the arts and trades. He gathered adults in them and trained blacksmiths, carpenters, masons, tailors and cobblers. He formed a whole group of painters, sculptors and jewelers who fashioned things for the churches and furnished them with crosses, holy vessels and other things.

He dominated the whole undertaking of schools. He founded a singing school and composed verses on the Christian doctrine for the use of his Indians. About 1530 he founded the school and hospital of San Jose for Indians in the City of Mexico.

He built an enormous church there. Before he died he had built a hundred churches.

His humility makes it impossible to sketch a portrait of him. His person is obscured by his work, and his letters are too modest to tell us anything about himself. And in his request of Charles V to send several religious of

Ghent to Mexico he gives evidence of a wonderful love for his Indians: "This way," he wrote "when I die the Indians will not miss me too much."

Archbishop Montufar would one day pay him an involuntary tribute when in a moment of exasperation he would exclaim, "Petro de Gante is Archbishop of Mexico, not I!"

Even today no name is more revered there.

V

The Twelve Apostles of New Spain

In the wake of the Conquistadors a stream of colonists had begun to flow across the Atlantic, but so also did a stream of missionaries. The friars came first, and among the friars the Franciscans. Father Olmedo was still living in May of 1524, to welcome the arrival at Vera Cruz of the famous mission of the Twelve, emissaries of Pope Adrian VI.

The Twelve arrived on May 13 or 14 at San Juan de Ulua. Their mission had been organized by the Spaniard, Fray Juan de los Angeles, who had offered to work among the Mexican Indians but in the Franciscan General Chapter at Burgos in 1523 had been elected General of his Order. He was always to hold the evangelization of Mexico dear to his heart, and the friars of this mission proved to be exceptional men. Friars Minor of the Observance under Father Martin de Valencia, Superior, there were nine priests, another religious who was ordained shortly after his arrival, and two brothers.

"The Twelve Apostles" were received with great honor at Vera Cruz. Their arrival meant the end of the beginning, the start of wholesale, methodical evangelization. They set out from Vera Cruz on foot for the City of

Mexico.

There are some stories told about their stops at Tlaxcala and Tetzcoco.

At Tlaxcala one of the priests, Fray Toribio de Benavente Paredes, heard the friendly Tlaxcala Indians repeating something about them. He asked the meaning of the word. "It means 'poor one' or 'poor ones,' Father," replied a soldier. Fray Toribio decided to take their name for him as his own and has been known ever since as "Motolinia." "The poor ones" had come to bring good news to the poor.

There at Tlaxcala they found Father Juan de Tecto. Seeing that he had not made much progress in converting the natives, Fray Martin de Valencia asked what he had been doing all year. "Learning a theology unknown to St. Augustine," replied Father de Tecto, "the language of these Indians."

At the Friary and school at Tetzcoco, Fray Pedro de Gante's students gave Fray Martin de Valencia a very interesting afternoon. When the facilities had been inspected, the boys were assembled to sing their hymns and Christian doctrine, which sounded rather odd set to the weird old Indian scores. It was clear enough that the boys enjoyed the singing, but Fray Martin thought they regarded it a little too much like play. Christian instruction was a serious matter. Then it was that Fray Pedro's great friend and counselor, Father de Tecto, replied to him that it was indeed serious, but that he should wait till he heard Fray Pedro actually instructing the boys. Fray Martin later found out that the boys knew Fray Pedro de Gante for a determined teacher, and that he had made the faith loved in their hearts.

Fray Martin and his religious arrived at the City of Mexico on June 17 or 18. On July 2, they held the prescribed chapter. Fray Martin was elected "Custos" or Guardian. The five Franciscans who had already been in Mexico, the three Flemings plus Fray Diego de Altamirano and Fray Pedro Melgarejo de Urrea, both with Cortes at the time of the conquest, received appointments along with the rest. Assigned to the chief provinces, the friars immediately began "to study the languages and to preach with the aid of an interpreter."[6]

Within six months after their arrival the friars began to preach not only through an interpreter but sometimes also by the written word. Once they began to understand the language they preached very often, "on Sundays and feast days and many times during the week...There were days when they preached two or three times."

When the friars "began to speak the native language with greater ease and were able to preach without manuscript," the Indians came in greater numbers. Almost at once they began bringing in their idols for destruction and asking for Baptism and catechism. One district one day and another another day, the Indians of Mexico City and Tlaltelolco began to assemble. The friars seem now to have devoted the weekdays to the instruction of the children. Christian doctrine and reading and writing went side by side. As the children progressed, the friars began to baptize them.

Because in the city it was very noisy and also because among the children of the Indian nobles receiv-

[6] History of the Indians of New Spain

ing instruction at the new Monastery were the little "lords" of Cuautitlan and Tepotzotlan, nephews or grandchildren of Moctezuma, these two towns were the first and second respectively, after the City of Mexico, to which the friars went.

After about a year the friars sent some of their number to Spain to try and secure the King's favor for the natives against the Spaniards, who were treating them like animals, and to recruit more friars. The land was big and the people many.

By the end of 1524, the Friars Minor had founded monasteries in two territories that were to become the principal fields of their activity, the Valley of Mexico and the region of Puebla. In each they had selected large native centers of the greatest importance and installed two houses. These were "in Mexico and in Tetzcoco, Tlaxcala and Huejotzingo." In the second year a fifth house was created, at Cuanhuahuac. In 1525 also, Fray Martin de Valencia opened a second school (after Pedro de Gante's) in Mexico City. But because they still knew little of the land and the language and had so much to look after in these towns where they resided, during the first two years, the friars seldom left them.

In the third year, however, people from other towns started coming in search of them, begging them to come to them too. When the friars went to their towns, "the Indians would set out to welcome them" on the way. When they got to these other towns, the friars would find the entire populace assembled and waiting "and their meal prepared." When they finished preaching "there were always some Indians to be baptized."[7]

[7] ibid.

Soon they were visiting many towns in a single day. The Indians were eager to learn, and once taught, they taught others.

The Mexican Church was created very quickly. Baptism was administered from the first with great facility. At first the missionaries had baptized mostly children, but soon the adults had begun to ask for it.

There was no formal catechumenate before Baptism, but no one was baptized without some kind of training. Of the sick all that was required was "sincerely to repent of their sins and to believe truly in the efficacy of the sacrament."[8] This was a reasonable procedure, "for these people," as Motolinia says, "with their fearful and timid character, were easily troubled, and some of them were so moved that they could not repeat a word of the prayers they knew perfectly."

It goes without saying that prebaptismal teaching was only for adults and children of some maturity. Also, the question whether to baptize babies at all arose only in the first years. As the country in time came almost completely under Christian influence, there began to be no objection to baptizing either them or very young children. As a rule, the Franciscans baptized babies only on Sundays after Mass, but the Indians were welcomed for this at any hour.

With regard to systematic instruction, the Franciscans devoted themselves especially to the teaching of the youth, for they realized that they were the ones who would be their best helpers.

[8] The Spiritual Conquest of Mexico

In each quarter of each village an elderly man was carefully selected to assemble the children of the workers every morning. He would bring them in a group to the church and take them home again after the catechism. This was after the pattern of a native custom. After Mass the children were brought together in the *patios* of the churches and separated into groups according to their knowledge of the catechism and the principal prayers. Afterwards they went home to repeat what they had learned.

The sons of the native aristocracy, since generally speaking at least, they were the future leaders of the country, were handled differently. The schools reserved for them were always attached to church and monastery. At first the Indians did not realize the importance of their instruction and were somewhat afraid, and the schools were not well attended. But soon, seeing the advantage of the friars' education, the nobles, instead of sending substitutes as they had been doing at first, sent their own children and actually insisted on their being admitted.

These boys lived in the monasteries as boarders. Morning and evening they studied the catechism, reading, writing and singing. They were taught to serve Mass and to assist the religious generally. They were taught silent prayer and made to discipline themselves.

Other very large schools besides Fray Pedro de Gante's were established, and some boys of humble parentage managed admittance. Also, the older and more advanced pupils taught the laborers, who came in their free hours in large numbers.

The children were docile, quiet, well behaved. They grasped their lessons well and helped one another. Some of them would develop into true apostles, and some would even become martyrs. The Franciscan historians would attribute to these youth the greater part, actually, in the conversion of the country.

Instruction was primarily moral, but also technical, and this latter soon created an elite of native craftsmen. In the City of Mexico and wherever there were friaries, the Indians produced the fineries they themselves knew and added to these the ones they learned from the Spaniards. Each year the work became more excellent.

For the first few years after the friars came, the Eucharist was kept only in the Friary of St. Francis in Mexico City. Then it was kept at Tetzcoco. As more monastery churches were built it was placed also in them. Pope Paul III directed that the Blessed Sacrament not be denied the Indians.

It was in the province of Tetzcoco in 1526 that the Sacrament of Penance was first administered. It was almost impossible to make the people understand it, and administering it meant great hardship for the friars, the hardest and most unremitting work involved in the conversion of the country. But little by little the Indians learned it.

Since there were not many confessors, where they found one they formed a path to him. The Indian who failed to confess did not consider himself a Christian. So it was a very ordinary occurrence, especially during Lent. And before all the principal feasts the Indians would write out their sins in the pictograph the friars had developed for communication at first and bring in their parchments for the priests to examine. The first monasteries were 40 and 50 miles apart, and if they had to to find a priest, the Indians thought nothing of walking nearly twice that. Motolinia said he had never seen Catholics more diligent.

Because of the Indians' timidity, the friars had to avoid everything which in the penitents' eyes might have seemed to be a criticism or reproach. The friars had to show themselves sorry for the sins the Indians confessed to teach the Indians to be sorry. Still, they gave absolution with great indulgence, and in order not to discourage their converts ordinarily imposed only light penances.

The natives were "by nature shy and very reserved..., so that when placed in a corner they stay there as if fastened down with nails. Many times they come to be baptized but are afraid to ask for the sacrament or even to speak." Many of them knew the Our Father, the Hail Mary and the doctrine, but when the priest asked that they recite them, they became nervous and didn't know what to say.

Motolinia would later write, "We have Lent all the year round. They come to confession at any hour of the day and in any place," even on the roads. The sick were very insistent. Their ailments rendered them more difficult. Since many of them had never confessed before, charity demanded that they be helped, like dying persons. Many were deaf. Others had sores. "The confessors in this land must not be too touchy and squeamish if they wish to hear confessions. Very frequently the sick are so numerous that the confessors resemble Josue asking God to make the sun stand still and lengthen the day...I firmly believe that those who faithfully persevere in devoting themselves to this work undergo a kind of martyrdom and render a service that is very meritorious before God..."

It was 1526 also that saw the arrival of the Dominicans. They too numbered twelve and were received by the Franciscans and housed in a modest temporary installation. However, five of them died the first year, and several others returned to Spain, till finally another contingent arrived.

Except in Tetzcoco where a procession was held with a simple Cross, up to the fourth year after the arrival of the twelve Franciscans none had been held. But before long they were being held everywhere. They were held throughout the year and brought together all classes and ages.

By 1528 the Dominicans were administering at least three native parishes.

All this time the friars were praying constantly. Fray Martin and his companions remained outstanding in their dedication.

In 1529 the Dominicans removed to the Monastery they had built for them. By about this time many of the Indians were becoming active, and with their help the friars were building churches everywhere. Many of the Indians were getting to Mass every day and receiving the sacraments often.

VI

Bishop Juan de Zumarraga

Even from the beginning, as well as throughout the entire colonial period, there were many great missionaries to Mexico. But from among them all must be singled out one man – the Franciscan Juan de Zumarraga.

He was born in the town of Tibira de Durango in the Province of Vizcaya in the Basque country of Spain about 1469 of a noble family. Two influences helped form his character, his good Christian home and his contacts with the Franciscan Friars who were frequent visitors. He seems to have been influenced also to some extent, at least in an educational way, by a close friend of the family, the Bachelor Arrazola. He also had some formal training at Valladolid, chancery seat of Vizcaya, before entering the Franciscan Order.

He probably entered the Order at the main convent of San Francisco de Valladolid of the Province of Santoyo. His affiliation with the Franciscans brought him into the main stream of the religious reform movement of fifteenth century Spain. He was educated according to the best standards of the day. He made his philosophical and theological studies prior to ordination in Valladolid, and it was a solid and thorough course in keeping with the strict reform of the Franciscans and the Spanish Church. He benefited by the insistence of Cardinal Ximenes on furthering scholarly pursuits among the Spanish clergy. He knew the writings of Thomas More and Erasmus and was not to hesitate to use those sections which he found applicable to the needs he would meet.

Some time after ordination he became "Guardian" or Superior of the Monastery of San Francisco de Avila and later of the house of Abrojo near Valladolid, at the time a noted center of humanism, learning and spiritual endeavor, a strict reform house. His discharge of his duties in the province got highest praise from the chronicler of the Order.

The important Province of Concepcion came into existence in 1518 from the fusion of the Province of Santoyo and the Custody of La Aguilera. He was made councillor of the new province that year and was elected Provincial by the second chapter. He served as Provincial from 1520 to 1523, about 26 months in all, of perhaps the most completely reformed province of Europe.

The life lived in the province emphasized silence, prayer, penance and poverty. After his term of office, he retired voluntarily to the convent of Abrojo. "He gave the rare example of a man being able to step down from the highest post to that of a simple father, and this in spite of his fifty-five years and the privileges accorded an ex-provincial. He was not left in this peaceful retirement for long."[9] He was named local Guardian, if not before, at least in the chapter of 1526.

He was Guardian in 1527 when Charles V passed

[9] Juan de Zumarraga, First Bishop of Mexico, D.J. Mulvihill, C.S.V., a dissertation, University of Michigan, 1954. This section relies heavily on this dissertation.

Holy Week at the Monastery. Charles was in Valladolid, for the General Cortes and ten years previously had also lodged there on his first arrival in Spain. He thus had occasion to assist at the Liturgy and to get to know the simple, sincere piety of Zumarraga and his religious. On leaving, Charles insisted that Zumarraga accept an alms. Zumarraga immediately gave it to the poor. This made a great impression on the Emperor.

Now by 1527, the Indian labor methods used in the Islands of the West Indies had almost destroyed the native population. During these years there was an ever increasing flood of petitions and complaints coming to Spain from that district. Among them were repeated requests that prelates be sent to regulate and direct the affairs of the Church there.

But it was too late to save the natives of the Indies. Still, "the useless waste that characterized the occupation of the islands must not be repeated...There was urgent need for a Bishop in the tumultuous capital of New Spain, where greed and lust ran riot and the helpless natives were being goaded to despair by insufferable abuses. The Indians were losing their land and being forced to labor at cruel tasks. They saw their daughters dragged off and their sons impressed into slavery and carried off to distant areas." [10]

Up to this time, the only diocese in New Spain was Carolina or Santa Maria de los Remedios of Yucatan, erected in 1519 by Pope Leo X with only the vaguest boundaries. The seat of this diocese was later transferred to Tlaxcala by Pope Clement VII, and this, properly

[10] The Dark Virgin

speaking, was the first Mexican diocese. The first Bishop was Fray Julian Garces, O.P., named in 1526. Later this episcopal seat was again transferred, to Puebla de los Angeles. Mexico (City) was actually the second diocese to come into existence on the mainland.

Charles, deciding to fill the need, sent instructions to his ambassador in Rome to seek the Papal approval of the appointment of Juan de Zumarraga as Bishop of Mexico. "This was in accord with the right of patronage granted by Alexander VI, by which the Crown had the right to select the candidates for ecclesiastical honors, the appointment resting with the Holy See."[11] At the same time, by another royal decree of the same day, December 12, 1527, Charles made known his intention to the humble Guardian of Abrojo. It was to prove a wise choice.

The decision to send Zumarraga right away, without waiting for the necessary bulls from Rome, "was dictated both by the urgent political and religious needs of the colony and the awareness at the Spanish Court that Papal approbation might be delayed for some time because of the strained relations existing in 1527 between the Emperor and the Pope."[12] The political relations between Spain and the Papacy were not too good. "The city of Rome had recently been sacked by troops of the Emperor." He and the Pope had finally ended their feud, and Charles had made a dramatic visit to Rome, but "the strain of the conflict had not been entirely relieved."[13]

To investigate charges of mismanagement brought

[11] "Don Fray Juan de Zumarraga, Pioneer of European Culture America, Alberto Maria Carreño, The Americas, July 1949

[12] Mulvihill

[13] Carreño

against Cortes an *Audiencia* or governing body had also been appointed, one day after Zumarraga, December 13, 1527, under a certain Nuño de Guzman, who had been Governor of Panuco. The *Audiencia* was similar to the one ruling in Santo Domingo, but with greater powers.

A sequence of events had led to near anarchy among the Spanish elements in New Spain, so that Cortes himself had been summoned back to Spain to answer the numerous charges made against him. A large part of the difficulty lay in the fact that as the first democratically elected white man in the New World, Cortes owed his authority more to the consent of his companions than to the King of Spain. He had sailed away to the conquest of Mexico and then emancipated himself from his superior, Diego Velasquez, the Governor of Cuba. He had later defeated and won over a punitive expedition sent against him by the latter and badly hurt its commander, Panfilo de Narvaez. As the result of representations to the Court of Spain, Cortes, on returning to the capital from a campaign, found his powers suspended. There was nothing to do but return to Spain to plead his cause.

Guzman carried an enormous authority, and Zumarraga had not been eager to accept. It took a positive command, on the insistence of the Emperor, from Zumarraga's religious Superior. He accepted the appointment as his "Cross and Martyrdom" only under obedience.

Charles also named Zumarraga Protector of the Indians. In part, in what concerns the civil laws of Spain, the origin of this office can be traced to the office of "Father of the Orphans" instituted by Peter II of Aragon who reigned from 1196 to 1213. Just what constituted the office is hard to define, but to the basic idea of the Bishop as pastor of his flock, it added the duty of teaching and caring for children who had lost their parents. "The immediate occasion for the creation of this overseas post was the result of the efforts of Fray Bartolomé de Las Casas and the interest that Cardinal Cisneros Ximenes displayed in the plight of the natives of the New World. Las Casas had been named the first Protector and various others nominated afterwards to this post.

"The office was a 'civil institution that had for its object to take under its patronage the natives of Spanish America, defending them against the oppression and mistreatment of the Spanish colonists and whites in general.'[14] Unfortunately, the government never outlined with sufficient clarity and judicial precision the rights and duties proper to the office...

"Authority was given to him to pass judgment on all crimes committed against the natives, and orders were given to all authorities in New Spain to carry out these decisions."[15] On January 2, 1528, Charles wrote, "... we command our president and auditors of the *Audiencia* of the Royal Chancery of the said New Spain, and our officials and other magistrates of the same, to give you and order to be given you all the support and aid that you should ask from them ..."[16]

Bishop-elect Zumarraga embarked on the same ship with the members of the *Audiencia* toward the end of August, 1528. After a journey of four months he arrived in Mexico December 6, a 60-year-old man and so sick that it took him a month in bed to recover. Two members

[14] Fray Juan de Zumarraga, Protector of the Indians," Fidel de J. Chavet, O.f.M., The Americas, January 1949

[15] Mulvihill

[16] Chavet

of the *Audiencia*, perhaps the better of the four under Guzman, died a few days after reaching the new land.

It may be debatable whether an iron hand was needed in Mexico during this period. But the *Audiencia* immediately began a positive persecution of all who had been loyal to Cortes. Then a savage program of extortion and enslavement was launched against the Indians. The only opposition was Zumarraga, Protector of the Indians and Bishop-elect, supported by the mission bands.

Immediately, Zumarraga opened his heart to the Indians. He received them freely and listened to their complaints. When he was warned against receiving "such foul smelling fellows," Zumarraga replied that the Indians had a heavenly smell to him, that they comforted him and gave him health.

He inaugurated a threefold policy: (1) to revive and stimulate the zeal of the clergy, (2) to curb the abuses of civil and military authorities and make the average settler realize the unchristian treatment accorded the Indians, and (3) to promulgate wide education and training for the Indians, particularly the children of the *caciques*, the former lords of the land.

Generally speaking the clergy responded enthusiastically, but Guzman and his associates refused to show Zumarraga the regard due a consecrated Bishop.

Zumarraga decided the only way he could carry out his office was to appoint inspectors and judges to study the complaints of the Indians and penalize their oppressors, with right of appeal, not to the *Audiencia*, but to him. He delegated certain religious as *visitors* to the different parts of the country to ascertain the causes of the abuses and the guilt of the perpetrators.

Guzman clamped down a strict censorship, put up a blockade between Mexico City and the port of Vera Cruz, and forbade both Indians and Spaniards to bring complaints to the Bishop. Then when Zumarraga presented his appointment as Protector of the Indians to the *Audiencia* in January 1529 in the company of Bishop Julian Garces of Tlaxcala, it was sourly objected that he had delegated his powers to the Franciscan Friars before doing this.

The situation was unfortunate, since both sides could claim legal justification for their actions, and no real solution existed except to render justice to the Indians.

But the *Audiencia* then sent its own investigators, relatives, friends or servants of the *oidores*, as the members of the *Audiencia* were called, who fleeced both the Indians and the Spaniards. This arbitrary stand of the very ones who had been appointed by the King to be his collaborators reduced the Bishop to helplessness. He denounced the *Audiencia* from the pulpit and declared he would take the case to the King.

He had the notice of the protectorate promulgated throughout the land, and the Indians were not hesitant in approaching him. They came to him at the Monastery of St. Francis in Mexico City, and the cases were so grave and the faults so numerous that he decided to try again.

He appealed to the *Audiencia* individually and as a group, but again was warned that these matters were not his concern. He was reminded that he lacked episcopal consecration and was only a simple friar no better than any other of the group then in Mexico and having no greater powers. The *Audiencia* forbade the colonists to aid Zumarraga in any way, and the Bishop was unable even to find a lawyer who would dare to counsel him. It was proclaimed also that no Indians were to consult him, and that if they did so they were to be hanged. An appeal for another meeting was denied, and Guzman went so far as to threaten Zumarraga's life. He told him that if he persisted he would suffer the fate of the Bishop of Zamora. The latter had been hanged.

The Bishop began to deal with the situation in his sermons again and had the other clergy do the same. Then the officials circulated among the people an attack on the characters of the Bishop and the Friars. The Bishop was refused a copy.

The Dominicans were partial to the *Audiencia*. Fray Domingo de Betanzos, Zumarraga's Dominican confessor, was transferred for a time to Guatemala.

The sermons and denunciations from the pulpit were followed by arrests and confinements to quarters. The threats of the gallows were countered by threats of excommunication. The Bishop's messages to Spain were confiscated. Indians in the service of the Franciscans were caught and tortured.

The climax came when some Indians from Huejotzingo, one of the former *encomiendas* of Cortes, smuggled a protest to Zumarraga.

An *encomienda* was an estate of land and the inhabiting Indians granted to Spanish colonists or adventurers in America for purposes of of tribute and evangelization. The system of *encomienda* was not unlike the feudal agrarianism of Europe. As early as 1529 Spain decided that the *encomiendas* should give way to *corregimientos*, or districts in charge of magistrates designated as *corregidores*. A realist, Zumarraga saw that the *encomienda*, in spite of the many opportunities it offered for abuse, was, if carefully regulated to safeguard the native, an indispensable stage in the ultimate incorporation of the Indian into the future Christian society that he was confident could be formed in the new land.

But these Indians of Huejotzingo were having such heavy tribute imposed on them by Guzman's lieutenants that they were obliged to sell their families into slavery to meet it. The Indians were forced to furnish the daily needs of all the members of the *Audiencia*. The great distances involved in the transportation of these foods required almost all the able-bodied men, women and children of the tribe merely to carry the daily loads to the city.

Zumarraga appealed again to the government, in vain. Surmising that the Indians had appealed to him, the *Audiencia* ordered the chiefs to be seized and brought to the city. The Bishop warned them, and they took refuge in the local Franciscan Monastery.

When the Bishop arrived at Huejotzingo he found the Franciscans both angry and discouraged. Some of them thought they should withdraw from the land as a body. They finally decided to remain but to have their most eloquent preacher, Fray Antonio Ortiz, attack the problem publicly by giving a well advertised sermon from the pulpit of the cathedral. Zumarraga was against it, but the majority decided for it.

On Pentecost Sunday, May 18, 1529, the Bishop of Tlaxcala celebrated Mass there. Fray Ortiz preached. Guzman's men curtly ordered him to stop his sermon. He continued "for the love of God and his Order." Having failed to shout him down, they dragged him from the pulpit. He had perhaps expected violence and made no protest.

Zumarraga having remained at Huejotzingo, the chancellor acted in his stead and pronounced the excommunication of the *Audiencia*. They ordered him seized and taken to the nearest port. He sought asylum in the church. The *oidores* contented themselves with guarding the building and forbidding anyone to bring him food. Zumarraga hurried to the city and imposed a minor penance. The *Audiencia* retracted the statements made in the public attack on the religious and burned the document. There followed a brief truce.

But the outrages against the natives were soon resumed.

As has been said, the *oidores* attempted a strict mail censorship. Still, the Bishop and Friars continued to try to get reports out to Spain. In August of 1529 Zumarraga decided to make the hard journey to Vera Cruz himself. The *procuradores* refused to carry the dispatches, but Zumarraga persuaded a Biscayan sailor to take them. The sailor hid them in a piece of wax and put it in a barrel of oil.

The letter displayed a calm dignity and a moral passion. Zumarraga did not appeal. He commanded that the King appoint a new *Audiencia* of honorable men, that he protect the Indians even under the *encomienda* system, and theat he put an end to all enslavement. Zumarraga cited the rumor that the King had given permission to enslave the Indians and told him, "If it is true that Your Majesty gave such a license, for the reverence of God do very great penance for it."

The King would heed the Bishop's advice, and Nuño

de Guzman would be dismissed.

Meanwhile the scandal that followed these and other events forced Guzman to get away from the *oidores*, with whom he was no longer on good terms. After disagreement within the *Audiencia*, in the fall of 1529 Guzman set out on about the 20th of December on an expedition for the conquest of New Galicia in the northwest. His absence did not help much.

Two winter months of the year 1530 passed without a further crisis, but on the night of March 4, the remaining *oidores* kidnapped two prisoners of the ecclesiastical court from the Monastery of San Francisco to the public jail where they were put in chains and subjected to torture.

Zumarraga learned of this latest outrage the next morning while offering Mass in the main church. He and his congregation could hear the cries of the victims. The Bishop took counsel with his legal advisors. Then, in company with the Bishop of Tlaxcala, he led a procession of clergy and laity bearing draped Crosses from the church to the gates of the prison. There he demanded the return of the two prisoners. The *oidores* ordered the large crowd to disperse. The Bishop ordered them to remain. The crowd rushed the gates, but their massiveness, bulwarked by the sharp weapons of the guards, was too much for them. Diego Delgadillo, in command now that Guzman was gone, again ordered the crowd to disperse, added several insulting personal remarks to Zumarraga. The Bishop replied in like manner. Delgadillo began to rage and ordered his men to clear the square with their swords. He himself led the charge and actually made a pass at Zumarraga with his lance, but missed him. There was no choice for the Bishop but to withdraw.

He placed the *oidores* under interdict, with the extension of the interdict to the entire city and decreeing the cessation "a divinis" if the prisoners where not returned within three hours. The answer of the *oidores* was on the morning of March 7 to hang and quarter one of the prisoners and to give the other a hundred lashes before cutting off one of his legs. The interdict therefore took effect for the entire city. The whole population was upset.

The Franciscans abandoned their church and Monastery in the city and installed themselves in their house at Tetzcoco with their young pupils, leaving the empty tabernacle wide open, the altars stripped, and the benches upset. It was in the middle of the Lenten season, and the people of the city were very much disturbed. The *cabildo* requested that the interdict be lifted, but the Bishop pointed out the fact that the *oidores* must come to him personally to be absolved. Innumerable negotiations failed, and the two *oidores* lost what prestige they still had. The interdict was suspended by law during Holy Week, and the Bishop never reimposed it, but the personal excommunication of the two men remained in force until 1531, until well after the coming of the new *Audiencia*. Satisfaction seems to have been no great matter.

By the spring of 1530, both sides knew that their reports sent the previous summer had reached the Court in Spain. The contradictory accounts of what had been happening far away in New Spain had caused some disturbance among the officials in the home country, but the Council of the Indies there had received enough information to believe the formation of a new *Audiencia* imperative. The Crown decided on a vice-regent. The Council of the Indies designated Antonio de Mendoza. As Mendoza could not go immediately, a temporary president was appointed, Don Sebastian Ramirez Fuenleal, Bishop of Santo Domingo. By April 1530, the president of the Council had selected Don Vasco de Quiroga, Alonso Maldonado, Francisco Ceynos and Juan de Saleron as the members of the new government. Quiroga would later be ordained priest and consecrated Bishop on the same day for the work he was doing in Michoacan.

Cortes returned to Mexico before the new *Audiencia* got there. He had been vindicated at Court and reached Vera Cruz with a large following July 15, 1530. However, his civil authority was greatly abridged in favor of the second *Audiencia*, and he was not allowed to enter the City of Mexico until the arrival of the *Audiencia.*

Zumarraga continued to work tirelessly to alleviate the evils of enslavement, until on August 2, 1530 the Crown ordered that from then on "no one should take in or out of war any Indian for a slave."[17]

The four members of the new *Audiencia* had arrived in Mexico by January 9, 1531 and the president Fuenleal by September 23. The second *Audiencia* faced a tremendous task, but its inauguration brought new hope to the country. A whole program of reconstruction was needed immediately to bring reassurance and stability to the terrified Indians.

But Zumarraga's conflicts with the state were not over. The Council of the Indies sent him a letter of August 30, 1530 in which he was told to obey the new

[17] Mulvihill

Audiencia or answer strictly for it. On instructions from the Council, the new *oidores* questioned him about his actions during the preceding years. Zumarraga's replies prove the man. On March 28, 1531, he wrote:

> "When they finally gave me the letter of your majesty ..., I told them (the *oidores*) that if I should be sentenced to be scourged as is the ass in the market place, and if I should be ordered to do a greater penance, I would not lose the satisfaction that I have in seeing the redemption of the land." [18]

He wrote another letter to the Council of the Indies at the same time and expressed in similar terms his resignation to any punishment they might decide on.

When the *procuradores* sent by the city and former government to Spain returned to Mexico with Fuenleal, they brought with them a royal *cedula* in which the Bishop was ordered to leave for Spain immediately. The main purpose of the summons was that the Bishop might report personally on the affairs of the colony and be properly consecrated, but it seemed to the friars as definite proof that the enemies of Zumarraga had enjoyed favor. "As for Zumarraga, he obeyed the command with the tranquillity of soul that was the result of his good conscience and willingness ... "[19] However, he was not to leave New Spain for more than another year.

In the meantime, the subjection of the Indians, though perhaps more "legal," hardly diminished. Even Cortes had his hands full trying to keep order among his

[18] Fray Juan de Zumarraga, Joachin Icazbalceta, II, No. 13, pp. 272-275, in Mulvihill, my parentheses.

[19] Mulvihill

Spaniards and enforce royal decrees. Distances were vast, roads practically non-existent, and Spain far away.

Still, on June 12, 1531, Zumarraga could write to the General Chapter of his Order:

> "Most Reverend Fathers:
>
> "...we are occupied with and engrossed in the great work of converting the unbelievers... more than a million souls have been baptized ...and in most places churches are now built...the Standard and Sign of the Cross is now honored and venerated by the Indians...(they) fast...and pray...many of these youths, and others who are older, already know how to read; they write and sing very well. They come to confession with much devotion and receive the sacraments...they teach others the word of God with much elegance...they...search out with diligence the places where their parents hide the idols and remove them...(they) bring them to the religious; for which deeds some of them have been cruelly killed by their own fathers...Each Monastery of our Friars has a house attached to it for the teaching of boys...These boys are very modest and obedient to the Religious, and love them as if they were their own fathers. They are chaste and clean...for the better education of the Indian girls, the Empress, Dona Isabel, sent out from Spain six fine and sensible women and instructed them to build a large house in which, under obedience to and with the support of the Bishop, they could teach a thousand young ladies. These

are now learning our Faith from these worthy *dueñas*, and the youths from the Friars, so that later they may in turn teach their parents.
Mexico, the 12th of June 1531"

The *cedula* ordering him to Spain was the last sign of royal displeasure Zumarraga incurred. The favorable reports which continued to reach the Court gradually dispelled the suspicions engendered by the criticism of the first *Audiencia* and its supporters.

In July of 1532, with nothing but his breviary and a pilgrim's staff, "on foot and without shoes," he left for Spain.

He was well received at the Court. However, Charles was at Ratisbon organizing his European defenses against the Turks; so Zumarraga didn't see the Emperor. He made a report to the Council of the Indies, which was a normal procedure for an official newly arrived from overseas. He seems to have answered satisfactorily, for he was allowed to go ahead with the ceremony of consecration. He was ordained Bishop on the Sunday after Easter, April 25, 1533 in the principal chapel of the Monastery of St. Francis at Valladolid by the Bishop of Segovia. The Court was at Valladolid, and the ordination took place "in great solemnity, honor and rejoicing." His legates were dispatched to Mexico to take possession of the diocese.

Shortly afterwards, he easily defended himself against Delgadillo before the Council.

He had begun a distinguished career.

But now it is time for us to turn to the events of December, 1531, of which we have not yet spoken. They are to shape the future of Mexico.

Chapter Two

Lady of Tepeyac

I

The Story of the Apparitions

Juan Diego was an Indian of the town of Cuautitlan about 16 miles north of Mexico City. Cuautitlan had been one of the most populous centers of the Aztec kingdom at the beginning of the conquest. Juan Diego had been born of humble parents, and his pagan name had been Cuauhtlocloatzin or Talking Eagle.

He and his wife, Maria Lucia, had been baptized by one of the twelve Franciscan apostles. After Baptism he had begun to be profoundly devoted to Mary, the Mother of God, so much so that he and his wife had walked the long miles from Cuautitlan to Tlaltelolco on the northern outskirts of Mexico City, where the church was to which he belonged, every Saturday at dawn to hear her Mass sung and the Christian doctrine expounded for the converts. He was gentle and straightforward, a simple and candid man with a pure conscience. He seems to have been in his late middle age.

The tradition holds that shortly after the husband and wife were baptized they had heard a sermon by "Motolinia," Fray Toribio de Benevente Paredes, in which he spoke of the excellence of continence and taught that "it was possible even in marriage ... "[20] They had decided to follow this rule of continence and from then on had lived in perfect abstinence. Fray Toribio must have spoken very effectively of Mary the Virgin.

In 1529 Maria Lucia had died. Juan Diego had then moved to Tolpetlac, a smaller village to the east and somewhat nearer to Tlaltelolco, to live with his uncle. He now walked to Tlaltelolco to Mass alone. He wore a cloak or *tilma*, made of *ayate*, a coarse fabric made from cactus fiber. It was well woven and was worn by the ordinary Indians, while the rich wore cloaks of cotton or wool.

Now let the Aztec document tell the story.

The Appearance of the Ever Virgin Holy Mary, Mother of God, Our Queen, at Tepeyac Hill, Guadalupe[21]

Ten years after the taking of the City of Mexico, when the war was over and there was peace among the peoples, the faith, the knowledge of the true God for whom we live, was beginning to germinate.

At that time, namely in the year 1531, a few days into the month of December, it happened that a poor Indian named Juan Diego, a native it is said of Cuautitlan but pertaining in spiritual things to Tlaltelolco, was that Saturday at early dawn headed there for divine worship and to do his usual errands. As he got near the hill called Tepeyac day was breaking, and he heard singing up on the hill.

20 "Our Lady's Messenger" Anonymous, from the Album of the Coronation of the Most Holy Virgin of Guadalupe, in The Dark Virgin

21 "Historia de la Aparicion de Nuestra Señora de Guadalupe," in...Hvei tlamahvicoltica...

It seemed to be the song of different kinds of precious little birds. Their voices ceased for a little, and it seemed as if the hills responded. Their song, very soft and delightful, surpassed that of other beautiful singing birds.

Juan Diego stopped to reflect and said to himself, “Can I possibly be worthy of what I hear? Am I possibly dreaming? Am I just now waking up? Where am I? In the early paradise the old people used to talk about, our grandfathers? Am I maybe in Heaven?” He stood looking into the east, toward the hilltop, to where the precious heavenly song was coming from. Then suddenly it stopped, and in the silence he heard someone calling him from the top of the hill, “Little Juan, little Juan Diego.” Then he boldly began to climb up to where he was being called from. When he got to the top he saw a Lady standing there. She told him to come nearer.

Having come into her presence, he was struck with wonder at her superhuman grandeur. Her garments were shining like the sun. The rock on which her foot rested, sparkling with splendor, seemed like an anklet of precious stones, and earth glistened like a rainbow. The mesquites, the prickly pear trees and the other scrubby plants growing there took on an emerald hue. Their foliage seemed like fine turquoise. Their branches and thorns glittered like gold.

He bowed before her, and listened to her words, which were very gentle and courteous, as to someone beloved and highly esteemed. She said to him, “Little Juan, my littlest son, where are you going?" He answered, "My Lady, my Little One, I have to go to your house at Mexico Tlaltelolco to attend the divine things which our priests, the representatives of Our Lord, teach us." Then she spoke and made known her holy will, saying, "Know and understand, O littlest of my sons, that I am the ever Virgin Holy Mary, Mother of the True God, for whom we live, the Creator to whom all is present, the Lord of Heaven and of the Earth. I urgently desire a temple to be built for me here, that in it I may demonstrate and grant all my love, compassion, help and protection, for I am your compassionate Mother, yours and all theirs who live together with you in this land, and all the others' my lovers who call on me and trust in me. Here I will hear their cries and heal all their miseries, sufferings and sorrows. To realize what my mercy desires, go to the residence of the Bishop of Mexico and tell him how I have sent you to lay before him my great desire, that here on this level he build me a temple. Tell him faithfully all you have seen and wondered at, and what you have heard. And be sure that I will show you my gratitude and reward you well, for I will make you happy and you will be very deserving of the great reward I will give you for your work and weariness. And now you have heard my command, my littlest son. Go and labor with all your might." Then he bowed before her and said to her, "My Lady, I will go immediately to accomplish your command. And now I leave you, I your humble servant." Immediately he descended the hill, to go and accomplish her command, and went off toward the causeway which led straight to Mexico City.

Having entered the city, he went right away to the Bishop's residence. This prelate had arrived shortly before and was don fray Juan de Zumarraga, a religious of St. Francis. Having arrived, Juan Diego tried to see the Bishop. He asked his servants to go and announce him. After a good while they came to call him, and told him the Lord Bishop said he should come in. As soon as he entered he bowed and knelt down before him. Then he related to him the message of the Lady of Heaven, as well as all that he had seen and wondered at and heard. When the Bishop had heard his whole speech, his whole message, he appeared not to give credit to it, and he answered, "Come again, my son, and I will listen to you more at length. I will look into this more thoroughly, and I will weigh maturely this wish, this desire with which you have come." He left. And he felt bad, for he had gotten his message across not at all.

That same day, he returned. He went straight to the hilltop, and met with the Lady of Heaven, who stood there waiting in the same place where he had seen her the time before. On seeing her, he prostrated before her and said to her, "Lady, my Littlest Daughter, my Little One, I went where you sent me to accomplish your command. Although I got into the prelate's residence only with difficulty, I saw him and gave him your message as you instructed me. He received me kindly and listened to me with attention, but from the way he answered it was obvious that he could not accept it as certain. He said to me, 'Come again. I will hear you more at length, and I will look into this desire, this wish with which you have come, more thoroughly,' I understood perfectly from the way he answered me that he thought that your desire to have a church built here was possibly my invention and not your will. I earnestly beg you, my Lady, my Little One, to entrust your message to one of the chiefs, someone well known, respected and esteemed. For I am a little poor man, a little piece of string, a little door step. I'm tail, I'm leaf. I'm common folk, and you, my Little One, my Littlest Daughter, you send me to a place where I am not worthy to be. Pardon me if I cause you a lot of trouble and fall into your displeasure, my Lady, my Mistress."

The Most Holy Virgin answered him, "Listen, my littlest son, there are many servants and messengers of mine whom I could entrust to deliver my message and do my will. But it is necessary that precisely you yourself urge this and help me and that my will be accomplished with your mediation. I urgently request you, my littlest son, and strictly command you, that you go again tomorrow to see the Bishop. Give him an understanding in my name, and let him know my whole will, that he build the church that I ask. And say again that I in person, the ever Virgin Holy Mary, Mother of God send you."

Juan Diego answered, "My Lady, my Little

One, I will not cause you grief. I will go with great pleasure to accomplish your command. Not one thing will I omit to do, nor do I mind the trouble of going. I will go do your will. It was only that perhaps I would not be heard with favor, or if I were heard, that I might not be believed. Tomorrow evening, at sunset, I will return to give you the prelate's answer to your message. And now I leave you, my Littlest Daughter, my Little One, my Lady. Meanwhile, rest confident." Then he went to rest in his house.

The following day, Sunday, at early dawn, he left his house and went straight to Tlaltelolco, for Mass and the instruction and to be present for the roll call, to go on afterwards to the prelate. About ten o'clock, having heard Mass, and been present for the roll call, and the people having dispersed, he was ready and left for the residence of the Lord Bishop. Having arrived, he did all he could to see him. Finally, with much difficulty, he did. He knelt at his feet. He implored him pitifully and wept, to get across to him the command of the Lady of Heaven. God grant that her message be believed, the will of the Immaculate, that her temple be erected where she showed she wished it.

The Lord Bishop, to make certain, asked him many things.Where did he see her, and what was she like? And he told all perfectly to the Lord Bishop. But although he described her figure exactly and all he had seen and wondered at, so that she came through totally as the ever Virgin, the most holy Mother of our Saviour, the Lord

Jesus Christ, nevertheless the Bishop did not give him credence and said that what he was asking for would not be granted simply because of his words and determination, but that besides, some sign would be indispensable to enable him to believe that the Lady of Heaven herself sent him.

When he had heard him, Juan Diego said to the Bishop, "Lord, wait here for whatever sign it is that you ask for, and I will go right away to ask the Lady of Heaven who sent me here." The Bishop, seeing that he stuck to everything without hesitation and went back on nothing, dismissed him. Immediately he ordered some of his people, whom he could trust, to go and follow and observe carefully where he went and whom he saw and spoke with. This they did. Juan Diego went straight, traveling by the causeway. The men who were following him lost him, though, when he passed the ravine near the bridge of Tepeyac. And although they searched thoroughly all over, they didn't find him. And so it was that they returned not only disgusted but frustrated and angry. They tried to influence the Lord Bishop not to believe him. They told him the Indian was just deceiving him, that he was just inventing that tale, or that at the most it was only a dream. In sum, they vowed that if he came again they would take him and discipline him harshly so that he would do no more lying.

Meanwhile Juan Diego was with the most holy Virgin, giving her the Lord Bishop's answer. When the Lady heard it she said to him, "It is good, my little son. Return here tomorrow to take to the Bishop the sign he has asked of you. It will make him believe you and no longer doubt or suspect you. And know, my littlest son, that I will reward you abundantly for all you have done for me. Well then, go now, and I will await you here tomorrow."

The following day, Monday, when Juan Diego was to take the Bishop a sign to make him believe, he did not return. For when he got back to his house, an uncle of his who was staying there, named Juan Bernardino, was very sick. First he had gone to get a medicine man and help for him. But there still had been no time, for he was gravely ill. Monday night his uncle begged him to go out the next morning and bring a priest from Tlaltelolco, to hear his confession and prepare him for death, for he was sure his time had come and that he would not get up or get well again.

Tuesday, early in the morning, Juan Diego left his house to go to Tlaltelolco to get the priest. And as he was nearing the hill, traveling along the road which passes Tepeyac Hill on the west, which was his usual way, he said to himself, "If I go straight ahead I can't help seeing the Lady, and she'll certainly detain me, to take the sign to the Bishop as I promised. Our affliction takes priority. First I must go get the priest. My poor uncle is certainly waiting for him."

Then he headed round the hill. He bypassed it, round the other side, the eastern, to get quickly to Mexico City without the Lady of Heaven detaining him. He thought that if he turned that way she would not be able to see him – she who sees clearly every turn; that she would not be able to see him who sees clearly the whole world.

He saw her coming down from the top of the hill, and stopped and looked up there to her, where he had always seen her. She came down the side of the hill to meet him, and said to him, "What's this, my littlest son? Where are you going?" Was he upset, or ashamed, or scared? He bowed before her and greeted her. "My Little One, my Littlest Daughter, Lady, God grant that you are well. How did you sleep? Are you feeling well, my Lady and Little One?

"I am going to cause you sorrow. Know, my Little One, that a poor servant of yours, my uncle, is very sick. He has the fever and is going to die. I am going quickly to your house in Mexico City to get one of the beloved priests of Our Lord to come hear his confession and prepare him for death. For from the time we are born we do but await the labor of dying. When I have done that I will come back here and take your message for you. My Lady and Little One, pardon me. Be patient with me for now. I'm not being dishonest with you, my Littlest Daughter. Tomorrow I will come right back to you."

When she had heard Juan Diego's speech, the most compassionate Virgin answered, "Listen and be sure, my littlest son, that there is nothing that should frighten or trouble you. Do not upset your heart. Do not fear this illness, nor any other sickness or heartache. Am I not here, who am your

Mother? Are you not safe in my shadow? Am I not your health? Really, aren't you in my embrace?" What else matters? Don't let anything upset or disquiet you. Don't let your uncle's illness bother you. He's not going to die of it now. Be assured that he is already well. (And at that moment his uncle got well, as he learned afterwards.)

When Juan Diego heard these words of the Lady of Heaven he was much consoled. He was easy and content. He implored her to send him again to see the Lord Bishop, to take some sign as a proof, so he would believe. The Lady of Heaven then had him go up to the top of the hill, where he had seen her before. She said to him, "Go up, my littlest son, to the top of the hill. There, where you have seen me and I have given you orders, you will find some flowers. Pick them, gather them all up together, and put them in your tilma. Then come back down and bring them into my presence.

Juan Diego went right up the hill. And when he got to the top he was quite surprised to find blooming there a great variety of exquisite Castilian roses, before their time, for the winter was then cruelly cold. They were very fragrant and full of the night dew, which seemed like precious pearls. He began to pluck them and gathered them all together and put them in his cloak.

The hilltop was not a place for any flowers. There were many rocks, thistles, thorns, prickly pear trees and mesquites. And even if any bushes grew there, it was the month of December, in which winter marred everything.

He went back down and took the roses he had picked to the Lady of Heaven. When she saw them she took them in her hands and arranged them again in his cloak and said, "My littlest son, this bunch of roses is the proof and the sign you must take to the Bishop. You will tell him in my name that he will see in them my will and that he must comply. You will be my ambassador, very worthy of confidence. I strictly order you that only before the Bishop shall you open your mantle and display what you carry. Relate everything carefully. Say that I commanded you to go up to the top of the hill, that you went to pick flowers. Tell him all you have seen and wondered at, to induce him to give his help, so that he will build the temple I have requested."

When the Lady of Heaven had spoken, he took the road to the causeway which goes straight to Mexico City. Now he was content and secure of succeeding. He carried very carefully what he bore in his mantle, that none of his precious load might fall out, and went glorying in the fragrance of the beautiful flowers.

When he arrived at the Bishop's residence, the steward and other servants of the prelate came to meet him. He asked them to tell the Bishop he would like to see him. But none of them would, pretending they didn't hear him, either because it was very early in the morning or because they recognized him, that he was only a bother, back to repeat his same request, or finally because the others of the household who had lost him on the road when they were following him had spoken to them about him. They kept him waiting there a long time. Finally, when he saw how long he was going to have to wait, he settled down humbly to be patient until he was called. And when they saw that he had something he was carrying in his mantle, they came up to him to satisfy their curiosity about what it was. Juan Diego, seeing that he could no longer hide what he was carrying, and that soon they would be giving him trouble or pushing him around and beating him, let them see some of the flowers. When they saw that they were all different kinds of Castilian roses, not at all in season, they were much astonished at them, the more so that they were very fresh and in full bloom, so fragrant and so precious. They tried to take some by force. But the three times they ventured to do so they could not. They were unable because when they went to take them they did not seem to be real flowers but appeared painted or embroidered or sewed on the mantle.

They went to tell the Lord Bishop what they had seen, and that the Indian who had come so many times wanted to see him, and that he had waited a long time. On hearing this the Lord Bishop realized that this was the proof that would satisfy him and enable him to comply with what the Indian requested. He ordered him to come in.

On entering Juan Diego knelt before him as he had always done and recounted once more all he had seen and wondered at, as well as his message. He said, "Lord, I have done what you ordered, told my Love, the Lady of Heaven, Holy Mary, precious Mother of God, that you required a sign in order to believe that she wanted you to construct a temple there where she requested it. And I told her I had given you my word to bring some sign, some proof of her will, of what she had charged me with. She graciously consented and looked favorably on your request for some sign or proof by which you might comply with her will. Early this morning she ordered me to come see you once more. I asked for the sign, by which you could believe me, that she said she would give me. She responded immediately and sent me up to the top of the hill, where I had seen her before, to pluck some Castilian roses.

"When I had plucked them I took them back down. She took them in her hands and arranged them again in my mantle, for me to bring them to you and give them to you personally. Although I knew well the hilltop was not a place where there were flowers – only a lot of rocks, thistles, thorns, prickly pear trees and mesquites – for all that I didn't doubt her. As I was approaching the top of the hill, it was wonderful. I was in Paradise. There were all different kinds of exquisite Castilian roses, brilliant with dew, and I immediately started picking them. She told me to deliver them to you. And now I have done it, so that you may see in them the sign you ask for and do her will, and also that you may appreciate the truth of my word, my message. Here they are. Take them."

Then he opened his white cloak, in which he

was carrying the flowers, and as all the Castilian roses fell out over the floor, there delineated itself on the cloak and suddenly appeared the precious image of the ever Virgin Holy Mary, Mother of God, as it is kept today in her temple at Tepeyac or Guadalupe.

As soon as the Lord Bishop saw it, he and all those who were there knelt to the ground and gazed with wonder. They got up to examine it. Then they grew melancholy and began to feel oppressed, which shows that their contemplation was of both heart and mind. The Lord Bishop prayed with tears of sadness and begged her pardon for not having put into effect her will and her command. When he had finished he untied from Juan Diego's neck, from which it still hung, the mantle on which the Lady of Heaven had appeared. Then he took it and placed it in his chapel.

All that day Juan Diego remained in the Bishop's house, for he did not want him to go. The next day the Bishop said to him, "Now! Show us where the Lady of Heaven wants her temple built." Juan Diego immediately agreed. Then as soon as he had shown them where the Lady of Heaven had commanded her temple to be built, he asked permission to go. He wanted to go now to his house to see his uncle, Juan Bernardino. He had been very sick when Juan Diego had left and and come to Tlaltelolco to get a priest to hear his confession and prepare him for death and the Lady of Heaven had told him that he had already been cured.

They did not let him go alone, but accompanied him to his house. When they got there they saw that his uncle was doing fine and that there was nothing wrong with him. He was much astonished that his nephew came with companions and a lot of honor. He asked why they treated Juan Diego this way and honored him so much. His nephew answered that when he had left to get a priest to hear his confession and prepare him for death, the Lady of Heaven had appeared to him on Tepeyac; that she had said he should not worry, that his uncle was already well, at which he was much consoled; that she had sent him on to Mexico City to see the Lord Bishop, in order that he might build a church on Tepeyac.

His uncle told them how he really was healed then and that he had seen her just as she had appeared to his nephew, and that he had learned from her that Juan Diego had been sent to Mexico City to see the Bishop.

Finally, the Lady had told him that when he should go see the Bishop he should tell him what he had seen and the wonderful way he had been healed, and that the most holy image of the Immaculate should be called

Holy Mary of Guadalupe, Ever Virgin.

+

Meanwhile, the word was out. Throngs of Indians surrounded the Bishop's residence, camping around it and even cooking their food there.

He moved the image to the Cathedral so that all the people could see it, whereupon the devotion became even more widespread in the city, so that the children were singing all about it in their games.

It seems that the Bishop and Cortes took up a collection, and the Bishop soon had a little one room adobe chapel built where Juan Diego had shown him the Lady of Heaven wished her temple.

Then on Christmas Eve Zumarraga wrote Cortes the following letter:

> "Illustrious Lord and very fortunate in everything.
>
> "Gratias agamus Domino Deo nostro. Let us give thanks to the Lord our God and resolve to serve Him even more from now on ... I am preparing for the (Christmas) festival, and for this reason I have kept the trumpeters and still have them; may Your Lordship please have patience for tomorrow and for the procession we are organizing (to the new little adobe chapel). You shall be richly rewarded on the joyous Nativity of Our Savior – and how glorious it will be! ... I have had the news published (of the image of the Virgin) and have made devotional visits to the first Monastery of St. Francis, to the Cathedral and to the Monastery of St. Dominic... And now for my procession... The joy of all is indescribable. I have sent a message to Cuernavaca to the Guardian. An Indian is already on his way to Fray Toribio, by all of whom may God be praised ... Laudent nomen Domini. The eve of the feast of feasts.
>
> "Will Your Lordship please tell the Señora Marquesa that I wish to entitle the Cathedral the Conception of the Mother of God, because it was at the time of her feast (within the octave of the Immaculate Conception) that it pleased God and

His Mother to show this mercy to this land which you won. No more for now.

"From Your Lordship's Chaplain,
He who was chosen to rejoice." [22]

On the day after Christmas, in a brilliant procession and after a very solemn *fiesta*, the Bishop installed the image in the new little chapel, and the devotion immediately spread throughout the whole capital area.

Word kept spreading. People began coming from as far away as Vera Cruz and Yucatan. Conversions started multiplying throughout the country. In the decade preceding the apparition, the cruelty of the Spanish soldiers had alienated the Indians, and Baptisms had been only about one million. But in the decade that followed, Baptisms took place en masse, to a total of something like eight or nine million. Teams of Franciscans and Dominicans working in pairs from dawn to dusk baptized whole districts. Churches sprang up all over the country, on the sights of almost all the old pagan temples. Under the direction of the friars, the Indians brought their ancient skills to the service of the True God and His Mother. They adapted their traditions to European forms and created a new style.

About 1555 the little adobe chapel would be replaced by a larger church. In 1663 the image would be moved to its first real temple. But these early buildings were like most of the rest of the churches in Mexico at the time, without window glass, though sometimes beautifully carved window shutters were a protection from the

[22] Album Historico Guadalupano Del IV Centenario, Mariano Cuevas, S.J. Translated by the author. Parentheses mine.

weather. Still, under even these poor conditions, the portrait would survive for centuries. In 1709 the image would be transferred again, to a sanctuary which would be its home until the 1970s, when a brand new contemporary basilica would be completed.

As for Juan Diego, from the day when the image was placed in the Virgin's first little chapel, giving his little houses and what lands he had inherited to his uncle, he left Tolpetlac for good. His neighbors built a little cell of adobe near the sanctuary for him, and there he lived quietly in seclusion like a hermit with Bishop Zumarraga's permission. He showed the sacred picture to pilgrims and repeated the story to them. He was "entirely consecrated to the service and worship of the Virgin, and (occupied) in provisioning and keeping clean the vicar's house. This he swept, and kept the little church sweet and clean; he prayed constantly and conversed with the Blessed Virgin familiarly, like a son with his Mother ... He was called the Pilgrim, because he always walked alone, and went abroad only to Tlaltelolco for religious instruction. He was an exemplary man, and a friend of all who lived decently.

"He spent long periods each day in prayer...While he lived he was so noted for sanctity that many who went to the Sanctuary to ask some act of mercy of the Blessed Virgin would ask him to intercede for them and include them in his prayers."[23] It became legendary for Indian fathers and mothers to ask a blessing for their children by saying, "May God treat you as He did Juan Diego."

At a time when the laity did not receive communion frequently, he had Bishop Zumarraga's permission to

[23] "Our Lady's Messenger" in The Dark Virgin

receive it three times a week. So he lived for 17 years while, as we shall see in some little detail, the millions of Baptisms were taking place. He died at the age of 74 in 1548, the same year as Bishop Zumarraga. His uncle, Juan Bernardino, died in 1544 at the age of 84. It is believed that Juan Diego was buried in the Virgin's little chapel.

"O Mexico!"

We have said that in the decade following the appearance of Mary eight or nine million Indians became Christians. Let us take a look at the work of her missionaries during that and the following decades.

"After Father Martin de Valencia and his companions had preached and taught eight years in Mexico (that is, about 1532), Father Martin wished to press onward to a region farther inland ... Certainly there is no true Christianity in the towns which the friars do not reach ..."[24]

In 1533, seven Augustinians were received by the Dominicans. By that time the Franciscans and Dominicans had founded many monasteries (by 1536 there were about 40 Franciscan houses), and the great roads to evangelization were no longer open. But there were still large areas that were untouched, and the Augustinians moved into them.

The first diocese in New Spain had been the Yucatan diocese, transferred to Tlaxcala in 1526, and later to Puebla. Zumarraga was appointed in 1528, and in 1537

[24] History of the Indians of New Spain

there was for the first time the consecration of a Bishop in Mexico, Don Francisco Marroquin for the diocese of Guatemala. In 1538, Zumarraga consecrated Vasco de Quiroga as Bishop of Michoacan and Juan de Zarate for Oaxaca. The Bishops referred to Zumarraga as "our father and consecrator."

The Franciscan mission, which started in 1525 as a simple custody attached to the Spanish Province of St. Gabriel d'Estremadura, became in 1535 an autonomous Province. The Dominican mission had in 1532 become the independent Province of St. James, while the Augustinians – in the beginning belonging to Castille – were formed into a separate Province in 1545.

The early beginnings had been modest enough, but afterwards the number of missionaries, though it was still too small for the population, increased quickly. Every year the vacancies caused by death and by returns to Spain were filled by a fresh contingent. Still, so great was the need, the Bishops, in a report to the Emperor, asked for even more friars, "a thousand if possible."

The Spaniards found the Indians very adept at the art of passive resistance. They would move to smaller remote villages where there were no missionaries to bother them and they could live as they pleased. Also, the Bishops saw the need of gathering into villages the scattered Indians in the even more remote hill sections of the country. Zumarraga wrote that if they were gathered together into such villages they would not diminish so much, for they were dying like animals in the wild, far from one another.

The friars went everywhere, trying to reach them,

holding discussions and teaching. They preached in Nahuatl and the other Indian languages. In whatever way it was done, the introduction of the Latin alphabet for the transcription of these native tongues was a revolution they effected in the intellectual history of Mexico.

They introduced music into the Liturgy, and the Indians were converted more by it than by preaching and came long distances to hear it.

The educational play, in which the Indians took part, was staged by the religious in the native language for the Indians alone.

The Augustinians had much confidence in the spiritual capacities of the Indians and had high ambitions for them. They seemed to be masters in the art of founding villages and administering them.

The missionaries taught the Indians better cultivation of their land and brought for the first time wheat and certain fruits such as oranges and apples, as well as cows and sheep.

In order merely to afford them time for instruction in the Christian doctrine, the friars had to struggle continually to free the Indians from the servile work, on Sundays and holy days of obligation, imposed on them by their Spanish overlords. It was the same with their efforts to obtain for them a lowering of the tributes which they had to furnish – constant struggle.

The Indians were so greatly in need of help that the friars could not help adequately. They had to be patient, perhaps mainly with the Spaniards, who themselves were forced to declare often that if it had not been for the Franciscans, New Spain would have been like the

Caribbean Islands where there was not an Indian surviving.

The missionaries lived so poorly that in 1554, the Viceroy Velasco would write to Philip II, "... as the Friars of this Order of St. Dominic eat no meat and always go on foot, their hardships are intolerable and they do not live long." They made a point of living as modestly as the humblest Indians. "They go about poor and barefoot as we do," said the Indians of the Franciscans. "They eat what we do, sit down among us, speak to us mildly."

The problem of recruiting was never exactly acute, but mortality was very heavy. The religious were frequently badly or insufficiently fed and prematurely worn out by excessive toil in an unhealthy climate.

The religious of Mexico knew that they had to speak their faith to the natives in the language of their example, and they spoke it even to death. "So we lost Fray Martin de Valencia, out of sheer penitence," wrote Juan de Samano in 1537. Bishop Zumarraga said Fray Martin "died of pure want."

He was not the only one. Fray Juan Bautista de Moya, for example, would not let anyone procure food from the Indians for him. He took so little that the Indians, who themselves got along on very little, were dismayed and wondered how he sustained himself. The Indians marvelled at the perseverance and the fortitude of the preachers, whose eating was so moderate.

The Indians for the most part had led a hard and miserable existence. Yet Suarez de Peralta could say of the religious, "They are almost worshipped by the Indians." Motolinia wrote, "One of the good traits of the friars here in this land is their humility ... Nor have the friars reason to be conceited when they consider the Indians, because the Indians surpass them ..." Yet the Indians recognized and respected their heroic efforts.

Many of the friars had come to New Spain with the desire for martyrdom. In 1540 Motolinia wrote, "Up till now God has not wished that any of them undergo the martyrdom of blood," but the following year the Franciscan lay brother Juan Calero and a companion were martyred by the Indians near Etzatlan in Jalisco.

Difficulties disturbed the evangelization and slowed it down, but they never dominated or stopped it, not even – that is to say, especially not – when they made martyrs.

There had been a point, though, when discouragement had almost triumphed. The friars had been on the point of giving up and returning home when providentially the Emperor Charles V and Pope Paul III had sent over 150 new religious from Spain. In 1540 Motolinia wrote likewise that more than 30 Franciscans had died in New Spain, but this large new contingent from Spain proved to stabilize and even bolster the situation.

As time went on more and more had come to be baptized, "not only on Sundays and on days set aside for Baptism, but also on every ordinary day – children and adults, the healthy and the sick." They came from all districts. When the friars would set out on their visits to Indian towns, the Indians would meet them on the roads with children in their arms and with the sick on their backs. Even the old and decrepit were brought. They would beg for Baptism on their knees and even with tears.

Including those who came on Sunday, there were weeks when three or four or five hundred children were baptized.

So many came to be baptized that "the priests who administered Baptism were often unable to raise the pitcher with which they baptized because their arm was tired." Sometimes a single priest would baptize on one day even four or five or six thousand Indians. Because the number of those who sought Baptism was so large, by this time the friars were setting out more often from the towns where they resided. Indians from many more towns were coming in search of them, asking them to come visit them, offering flowers and chocolate, a favorite beverage, especially in hot weather. Many came a two or three day's journey, "The lame, the blind and the mute, enduring great hardship and hunger ..." On one day the friars would visit and baptize the Indians of three or four towns. Soon, two by two, the Franciscans were visiting many more districts. Christianity expanded and became deeply rooted.

In the end, Motolinia could write, "It is worth seeing how quietly the Indians are enjoying their farms and with what solemnity and gladness the Most Holy Sacrament is venerated, how solemnly the feasts held in its honor are celebrated ... A town in which the Blessed Sacrament is newly placed invites to the prepared feast the neighboring and friendly towns ..."

The Blessed Sacrament was placed reverently in well made silver monstrances. The tabernacles were decorated within and without very gracefully with beautiful gold and featherwork, "of which in this land there are many first-class experts."

By 1540 Mexico formed for the most part a well established Christian community in which the Indians led "a peaceful and quiet life ..."

Motolinia declared that all were now "so right-minded" that a man laden with bars of silver could travel hundreds and hundreds of miles "over mountains and sierras, through populated and unpopulated districts" with no more fear than he would have walking down the main street of a town in Spain.

Mexico City itself was entirely surrounded by high mountains, "a very beautiful crown of ranges." The fact that the city lay in the center of this crown lent it charm as well as great security. It harbored the Divine Presence in the Blessed Sacrament of the Eucharist in many churches. In the main church resided the Bishop with his dignitaries. The church was very well administered and equipped. In the friaries there were many good religious. From these friaries missionaries continued to issue forth to preach in Spanish and many of the Indian languages.

"O Mexico," wrote Motolinia, "that such mountains should encircle and crown you! Because the Faith and Gospel of Jesus Christ shine forth in you, with reason will your fame now spread. Previously the mistress of sin, now you are the teacher of truth. Formerly in darkness and obscurity, now you give forth the splendor of Christian doctrine and civilization ... in other times ... You were a Babylon, full of confusion and wickedness; now you are another Jerusalem, the mother of provinces and kingdoms. Then you went whither it pleased you ...; now many are watching over you, taking care that you live according to divine and human laws ...; today ... you adore and profess the Lord of Lords. O Mexico! If you would raise your eyes to the mountains that encircle you, you would see more good angels aiding and defending you than formerly demons stood against you ..."[25]

[25] History of the Indians of New Spain

Conclusion

Mary: Virgin, Mother, Queen – Lady Obedience

In the sixteenth century of our era, the sublime Lady of Guadalupe found her beloved Mexican people in a condition that was perhaps one of the most miserable within the experience of men. But she taught them that, although sadness, suffering, pain, agony even – evident on every page of the human epic – are in fact sometimes only too very real a part of it, they nevertheless can be made to be "according to God." In teaching them love, she taught them joy. In giving them herself, she gave them the gift of song.

Their devotion to her forms the most basic factor in the country's culture. It is the single factor that united all these hostile and suspicious tribes. It is the only explanation for the survival over the centuries there of the true faith of Rome. Without the phenomenon of Guadalupe, the Church would never have become in Mexico anything like the force it now is.

It may perhaps be something of an oversimplification to say that "private revelations" contain nothing new, "no new truth," nothing that is not to be found in the deposit of public revelation. For when approved by the Church, they can offer vital insights into Divine Truth that the Church might otherwise never have attained to. One thinks, for instance, of Fatima and the objective importance of the Rosary.

Here at Guadalupe, though, there are no conditions, no "threats." Mary says simply: "Come to me. I am your Mother. I love you. I will comfort you in your sufferings and heal you." Surely, more than any other, this is the message we need today: I will heal you, I will make you whole.

In any case, and whatever kind of miracle Guadalupe is, it is a most wonderful *wonder*, direct from the Holy Spirit and Mary, the Mother of God, His Bride. She did not appear "out of due time," but only after the missionaries had been laboring for ten years to set the stage for her. Nor, once having come, did she stay to do all the rest of the work herself. She left her image, as a sign that she would accompany and bless the fatiguing, heroic labors of the religious men and women who were working already in her cause and the cause of the Lord, the God of all men. Nevertheless, it is still true to say, "Non fecit taliter omni nationi." He hasn't, she hasn't done this for every nation. Mexico, and all we Americans who cling round this gift to Mexico, are privileged; though in a broader sense, of course, He did it, she did it, for *all*.

Yes, and this is my thesis, that Guadalupe is for everyone. The Virgin of Guadalupe alone forms the link among all the American peoples, all the peoples of the western hemisphere. But in this unity of the western hemisphere, to a great extent, lies the hope of the whole earth. "While the Americas stand together, strong and steadfast, the last hope that peace shall again prevail in all the world is not lost."[26] That hope rests on faith in this Lady, and the God she brings us in her Son.

And in this unity – first, of all the Americas, but by their instrumentality, of the whole human family – lies the final meaning of the grace, the highly refined, contemplative beauty, the mercy, and the fidelity, but above all, the intense and overwhelming love of the Virgin Mary of Guadalupe.

Yes, Guadalupe is solid. When the Second Vatican Council became hung up on the schema on the Sources of Divine Revelation, Pope John XXIII paid a visit to the image of the Virgin of Guadalupe in the Mexican College in Rome. He came away with the answer. The discussion was postponed until the Assembly should be ready for it. It had been the critical moment of the Council.

And Pope John Paul II's first journey as Pope was to this shrine of Mary's in Mexico. It was as if she were most lovingly requiring him to visit first her special sanctuary where she reveals herself to all as "the grace of Christ the Redeemer ... a woman clothed with the sun." [27]

O Virgin of Guadalupe, you are the true riches of America! Mother of Fair Love, of true fear, of knowledge, and of the Holy Gift of hope, where sin abounded you abounded more! You are truly the Virgin of the Poor.

Virgo clementissima – Virgin most merciful ...

O Mary, yours is a virginity so fruitful, a humility so truly beautiful that you have become an inexhaustible

[26] The Grace of Guadalupe, Frances Parkinson Keyes, Burns Oats and Washbourne, Ltd.

[27] Pope Paul VI, Apostolic Exhortation, "Signum Magnum"

treasure to men. Whoever discovers this treasure that you are wins the friendship of God. (Wisdom 7, 14)

In giving us yourself, you give us the Gift of God, for in your own most sublime holiness you bring us the Holy Spirit. Why is it, Lady, that you are so often thought of as someone who merely helps us to salvation, gets us out of purgatory "on the first Saturday"? *You are a sanctifier!* Who kindle burning, holy love – the Holy Spirit Himself, the Sanctifier – in our hearts and souls, and make us saints. This is the devotion to you that I want to spread. If love has anything to do with it, I haven't the slightest intention of going to purgatory. When I die, I will fly straight to your waiting and outstretched arms. O Mary! You will rather come and take me with you to the Kingdom of Eternal Joy. In the meantime, dear Lady, my heart aches for you. Yet I have your peace.

There is no need to be afraid, either of sin or of mediocrity, for you, O Mary, will keep your beloved children from both, for you, are *par excellence* the instructress in love and virtue, always present to us, even when we are temporarily not expressly thinking of you. Mother of God, to begin with, I believe that no one who ever called on you even but once in his or her whole lifetime has been lost. But I believe further that you have made every single saint what he or she is. Lead us all as quickly as possible to most perfect love. Come to us soon, in the company of Him who is "coming quickly." And until you come, grant that we may bear you in our heart, and so walk safely and securely.

Gentle Lady, lead us all to our Lord Jesus Christ.

When a person prays just one little prayer to you,

Mary, that one thing leads to another, and before he knows it, he's heels over head in love with you, all because you heard and favored that one first prayer, a tiny, silent cry in the night, it may have been. And so we cling to you, Mary. Show us Jesus as even more attractive, infinitely more attractive, than your ravishingly beautiful self. Teach us not to hate life and love death, in the name of "religion," but with true faith, *real* faith, to love and find eternal life even here and now.

We need you, Mary, not because Jesus is a stern judge, but because His love is too much for us to comprehend without your gentle assurance that it is truly He. We need you, not so much as an advocate or mediatrix as such, but as a support, a secure harbor, a haven, a refuge to return to when the Mystery of His Love becomes too overwhelming for our minds to take "straight." When that love rushes on us we lose all foothold, as it were, and it is you, Mary, who gently teach us not to be afraid to let go of all hold and abandon our hearts and entrust ourselves absolutely to the Mystery. His love is so great that we feel terribly lost all over again and with a frighteningly increased sense of displacement at each new advance of it. We are like a girl getting to know a boy, little by little surrendering our autonomy and advancing into a great unknown experience. It's all so big.

Mary, you are the image of God's goodness. You can do all things. (Wisdom 7, 26-27) Whoever loves you loves life. Whoever seeks you out wins your favor. Those who love you the Lord loves. (Sirach 4, 12-14) Whoever obeys you dwells in security, in peace, without fear of harm. He will not be put to shame. Whoever serves you serves the Holy One, and will never fail. (Sirach 24, 21; 4, 14)

O Mary, I want to pray to you. Come visit me with peace and love. Come visit me simply with your wonderful presence. I kiss your feet, not because you want it or need it, but because *I* do. And you permit it. My Lady, sometimes I don't even think of God – I am overawed merely by the splendor of your own greatness. Yet I pray, lead me to Him. I choose you, Mary, and you give me the true Christ, the one real Truth who is before and above all else the Child of your womb, the Son of Mary.

"Mary is a certain armor of salvation which God gives to those whom He wills to be saved," said St. Ambrose. O Lady, I kneel before your statue. A little brown moth lands too. Together we make our prayer. Mary, Queen and Mother of All things, hear us.

I look down, and the little moth has moved over to the center of the statue, at the foot of the base. It's a smart little moth. It knows that the securest place in the universe is at the feet of this Lady. It just waits there. The Blessed Mother will take care of it.

Wise little moth, teach me confidence.

O Mary, Lady Humility, teach me your own humility, the humility of love. And she whispers. "Believe, even without seeing. Be faithful..."

Another day I am kneeling here, kissing the feet of her statue. It is December 26, and it is cold. I think so to myself. But she says to me, "I want you to kneel here for a few minutes in the cold. I have something to tell you." I wait, with head bowed, and ask, "What, Mary?" Then she says, "I love you."

In the cold? What cold?

Conform to the will of Mary, for God "never refuses the prayer of His dear Mother, because she is always humble and conformed to His will."[28] And besides that – there will be wonderful surprises...

Virgin of the Temple,Virgin of Nazareth, Virgin of Bethlehem, Virgin of Egypt, Virgin of Jerusalem, Virgin of Ephesus, Virgin of Patmos – O Mary clothed with the sun, be the only woman in my life! All my hope is in you. I have given up all hope of salvation or sanctity or the next meal or *anything* except through you and from your hands and by your will and in your way.

I was reading the Gospel of the Canaanite woman, "the Gospel of a mother's prayer" – for her daughter. She prayed, "Have pity on me, O Lord..." He answered her not a word. His disciples tried to get Him to send her away. He said He was not sent to people like Canaanites, which must have been the truth, but it certainly must have hurt. He entered a house, "but she came and worshipped Him." She said, "Lord!" And to me there is a world of pathos, beauty, suffering, prayer, humility in that entreaty. He said, "It's not fair to give the children's bread to the dogs." And we know her answer, and His admiration of it.

O Lady Mary, obtain for me the "great faith" of this woman, who is a figure of you.

And as soon as I make my prayer, immediately I hear Jesus say to Mary, and through Mary to me, "Let it be done to you as you will." (Matthew 15, 21-28; Mark 7, 24-30)

[28] True Devotion to the Blessed Virgin Mary, Louis de Montfort

Devotion to Mary, and the little tiny way of spiritual embryogenesis. O Mary, the Embryonic Christ is hidden in the depths of your womb. The Church is your mystical womb, "the fullness of Him who fills the whole universe." Thus the Embryonic Christ is the Christ maturing throughout the whole of the cosmos.

"A great sign appeared in the sky, a woman clothed with the sun, and the moon was under her feet, and upon her head a crown of twelve stars. Because she was with child, she cried out in pain as she labored to give birth." (Revelation 12, 1-2)

"The LORD has created a new thing upon the earth:
the woman must encompass the man with
devotion." (Jeremiah 31, 22)

You, Mary, are the woman who encompass us all with transcendent devotion, until you bring us all to birth definitively as the Body of Christ in Heaven. We are the embryonic Jesus, within your mystical womb, the Church.

O Mary, in you "I live and move and have my being." You are my pleasant atmosphere, in which I find life sweet and gracious. Mother, make me worthy of your gift.

I've heard and read, dear Lady, that possibly you came from a somewhat well-to-do-family, while Joseph was only a poor carpenter. But what did you care for the wealth of this world when you could have the love of Joseph? Of course, for all this, it was still he who was blessed immensely the more when you for his sake and ours became poor. You became not merely the Virgin of the Poor, but the Poor Virgin. Still, it was all for love.

And indeed, the Mystery of Christ is precisely this Mystery of Nuptial Love – of God and His Bride, Mary, and the church in Mary, symbolized by the union of Mary and Joseph. For Mary, as the perfection of the Church, is the Bride of Christ *par excellence*. How utterly beautiful! Yes, only in Mary is the Church the *absolutely* spotless bride of Christ.

But it is Joseph who is our teacher with regard to the Mystery of Mary the Bride. He better than anyone else could have spoken these words of wisdom:

"When I was young and innocent," I sought Mary.
"She came to me in her beauty ...
"My feet kept to the level path
because from earliest youth I was
familiar with her ...
I became resolutely devoted to her– ...
I burned with desire for her ...
never weary of extolling her."
For her I purified even the soles of my feet.
"... in cleanness, I attained to her.
At first acquaintance with her, I gained
understanding
such that I will never forsake her.
My whole being was stirred as I learned about her;
therefore I have made her my prize
possession." (Sirach 51, 13-21, passim)
As for me,
"Beyond health and comeliness I loved her,
And I chose to have her rather than the light,
.....
Yet all good things together came to me in her

company,
and countless riches at her hands;
.....
For she is fairer than the sun
and surpasses every constellation of the stars.
Compared to light she takes precedence;
for that, indeed, night supplants,
but wickedness prevails not over" [Mary.]
.....
"Her I loved and sought after from my youth;
I sought to take her for my bride
and was enamored of her beauty.
.....
even the LORD of all loved her.
For she is instructress in the understanding
of God,
.....
So, I determined to take her to live with me,
knowing that she would be my counselor while
all was well,
and my comfort in care and grief.
.....
For her sake I should have immortality
.....
Within my dwelling, I should take my
repose beside her;
For ...
living with her ... / [is] joy and gladness.
Thinking thus within myself,
and reflecting in my heart
That there is immortality in kinship with" [Mary,]

"and good pleasure in her friendship,

.....

And that in frequenting her society there
is prudence,

.....

I went about seeking to take her for my own.

.....

And knowing that I could not otherwise possess
her except God gave it –
and this too was prudence, to know whose is
the gift –
I went to the LORD and besought him..."

give me Mary, the Mother of the Word, to be my Lady and Queen! (Wisdom chs. 7 and 8, passim)

And in answer to my prayer, it is Joseph who says to me,

"If one trusts" Mary, "he will possess her;

.....

at first she puts him to the test;
Fear and dread she brings upon him
and tries him with her discipline;
With her precepts she puts him to the proof,
until his heart is fully with her.
Then she comes back to bring him happiness
and reveal her secrets to him." (Sirach 4, 16-18)

He concludes,

"Submit your neck to her yoke,
that your mind may accept her teaching.
For she is close to those who seek her,
and the one who is in earnest finds her."
(Sirach 51, 26)

O my Lady Mary, yes, yoke me to your discipline! For happy is the man who meditates and reflects on you, who ponders your ways in his heart, who pursues you, and lies in wait at your entry way, who peeps through your windows and listens at your doors, who takes shelter with you from the heat, and dwells in your home. (Sirach 14, 20-23 and 27)

Mary, I seek you. Scripture says that, mother-like, you will come to meet me, like a young bride you will embrace me. (Sirach 15, 2) Sweet Lady, how I long for it! You know, Mary, "a man with no wife becomes a homeless wanderer." (Sirach 36, 25) O Mary, this is how badly I need you! I need you for my spiritual bride. Surely I'm not wrong in this. Surely you are pleased with this desire of mine, to wed you mystically ...

O my lovely Lady, give me lilies for my Lily! Orchids for my Orchid! Every kind of flower for you, who are the Fairest Flower of Paradise!

O pretty Lady, you surrendered to Joseph in a very real way. You surrendered your whole physical being into his loving care. You depended on him completely, though, of course, ultimately it was he who surrendered to your surpassing virtue. O Mary, wound my heart, as you wounded his, with an incurable wound of love. Beautiful Lady, be the death of me!

It seems to me really dumb for people to deny that your love for Joseph, Mary, and his for you, took the form, in part, of physical attraction. It was under perfect control, of course, due to your fullness of grace and Joseph's great holiness, from the womb, as theologians say. But this attraction must have been greater than any other couple has ever known or ever will know. Did it not make you both very, very happy, Mary, and humble Joseph beyond words – and sanctify him, from the moment he first saw this divinely wonderful young girl, and fell in love with her heavenly beauty?

O Mary, if it be God's will, grant that I may lay down my life as Joseph did, in witness to your perfect and perpetual virginity.

Mother of God, when Jesus was born in that stable in Bethlehem, Joseph must have been everything to you. He must have held your hand and delivered the Baby and loved you as no one less than God Himself ever has or ever will.

There is the story of St. Maximilian Kolbe that when he was a boy you appeared to him with two crowns in your hands, one red, for a martyrdom of blood, one white, for a martyrdom of chastity. You asked him which he would like. He answered "Both." You smiled and vanished – and granted him both. O Mary! Crucifixion inside out – a red, white and blue martyrdom – this is the gift I ask of you according to God's will, crucifixion inside out, on a Cross of absolute fidelity.

The great St. Louis de Montfort wrote that those who practice true devotion to you don't have to go through all kinds of terrible "dark nights." I would not think of denying this. Yet if we are to be glorified with Christ, we must suffer with Him. Therefore, perhaps we may take this statement of his "with a grain of salt." But certainly, life and death – and dying – with you, Mary, are infinitely more human, and the darker the night the nicer it is to spend it with such a lovely Lady. At the time the darkness may seem utterly terrible. Yet you are always able to say to us in most perfect truth and realty, "You will remember me as sweeter than honey." (Sirach 24, 19)

Truly, my Lady Mary, "Your voice is sweet,
and you are lovely." (Song of Songs 2, 14)

O Mary, lay on me a man's burden, the burden that Jesus and Joseph bore, Joseph, *virum Mariae*, as the Gospel says, "Mary's man." St. Joseph, teach me. But above all, You yourself, Lord Jesus, help me to live and die for my beautiful Lady, just as You did.

I am inconsistent. My faith is troubled by the apparent desolation of the deaths I have seen, and yet I still go on protesting that I wish to be crucified for your love, Mary. Mother of God, only be with me to the end, and I will have in fidelity to you – as perfect as possible – all the crucifixion I can handle. Your love will triumph. Your Heart will triumph. *You* will triumph, in whatever may happen to me, whatever may be my fate. You will stand at the foot of my tiny Cross, sweet Lady, and it will be my unspeakable happiness to suffer and die on it for your love.

Exquisite Maiden, let me die nobly for your virginity, that your Beautiful Love may live in the hearts of men. Mother of Martyrs, be my Mother – our Mother. Once again, I choose you. Be for me that "best part" which will never be taken away from me. Do with me, Mary, what in some sense you couldn't do without me. Use me, for the salvation and sanctification of all – for the Christianization of the world and the humanization of the Church.

"Woman, there is your son." – "The son of Zebedee

for the Son of God!" cried St. Bernard. And yet the son of Zebedee was also a son of God, and, Mary, you had the immensely great faith and love to accept and embrace him as such. You did not pity yourself for losing a divine Son and having to be satisfied with a poor, merely human replacement. You did not consider John a relatively miserable substitute. Your love was so selfless that from the moment the words of Jesus sounded to you from the Cross, your strong and most holy Heart went out to John in compassion for his need, his weakness, his bereavement. He was orphaned, and you would take him into your Heart's care, while he took you as his own *everything*, all that was left in this world to his poor, perhaps not much more than adolescent heart.

The reason Jesus loved John most of all the Apostles was that John was the youngest, probably not much more than a teenager; a "son of thunder," a young man on fire with zeal to reform the whole of human society. When the world of all his magnificent ideals collapsed and his wondrous Leader ended up hanging from a Cross, his soul, his dreams, his purpose, his "goals," as the psychiatrist would say today, were all shattered and swept out from under him in the flood of this dirty, evil world's apparent triumph. He had fled with all the rest, but he had fled to you, Mary, and you led him to the foot of the Cross.

He got his reward, his salvation, his doctrine, his answer, from someone who understood the meaning of "AGAPE," the Love of Wonder.

Standing at the foot of the Cross and never collapsing, you must have sustained the equivalent of the most complete "nervous breakdown" in the history of the world, and it was for this reason that the disciple took you into his care. (John 18,27) Yet since John himself was only an orphaned youth, you and he together must have made a pitiful picture, such as we sometimes see in this sad, sad world, where so often the wretched can find help only from others as wretched as themselves.

Many praise your faith and humility, Mary, but I prefer to speak of your *love*. Yes: There stood by the Cross of Jesus Mary, His Mother. You teach us that love is nothing other than fidelity, absolute, even to death.

O Mary, I want to be your knight, as Jesus was. May I call myself the Knight of the Virgin Mary? You are the true Queen under whom I fight. It's true, I'm not much on horseback, and I can't handle a sword very well, but still I can't wait to meet that dragon for your love, even if it's with nothing more than a slingshot. O Spouse of the Holy Spirit, I love you.

If I am the knight of the Virgin Mary, may it not be possible, Lady, that by my suffering and love I may be able to free you from some slight degree of distress that would otherwise have gripped you as you stood broken but erect at the foot of the Cross? If you were preserved free from every blemish by the foreseen merits of Christ, may you not perhaps be preserved free of some little hurting at the foot of the Cross by the belated desires of my poor heart? Make it so, dearest Lady, make it so.

O Mary, I would change all your sufferings into joys, all your tears into smiles. I'm a sinner, but still I love you and want you. Form me in humility and confidence.

If I say, "I love you, Mary," should it mean that I

would go out and die for you? I can't do anything without your help, and I feel more like your clown than your warrior. When I say, "I love you," what does it really mean? "To each of us, whether righteous or sinning, Mary could say as she once said to St. Alphonse Rodriguez, 'I love you infinitely more than you love me.'"[29] What does it mean then?

I have no faith in my own reliability, Lady, as something apart from your gift. Indeed, it does not exist. And yet, though I know that I am no more than a second rate thinker and perhaps no more than a third rate writer, yet I know too that you are able to make of me a first rate lover. That is what it means, Mary. It means I want to love you as you have never been loved before or ever will be again.

O Mary, you are for me somehow "the sacrament of Christ." I chose the hardest when I chose the most perfect in choosing you. But ever since then I've been choosing the easiest, in spite of myself. Since I am too cowardly to choose suffering, I choose fidelity – to you. And is not this to choose all things?

You are my virtue, and I am – what, Mary? Am I not your responsibility? You make me speak to you in faith, but you say to my heart, "I will never abandon you."

I believe it, Mary, even when I seem to be abandoning you. When I fall, when I misbehave, when I am unfaithful, you simply take away my happiness until I return to you. For you *are* my happiness. When I am with you, I am fully a man. You are always with me, even

[29] The Virtue of Trust, Paul de Jaegher, SJ

when I fall. O my Lady, may my falls glorify by sheer contrast the transcendent beauty and greatness of the virtue of your soul. You *are* virtue, Mary, and I am only need of you personified.

I need you, Mary, and I want to need you, and I delight to need you. You are virtue, and I am need. I'm a hypocrite, a heel, a coward, false and faithless. Yet I love you, Beautiful Lady. Have mercy on me. I don't want to fall, but it seems that I will go right on falling anyway – and returning to you. Take everything from me, Mary, and so make me come to you for everything. Take everyone, that I may find everyone in you alone. I'll never have any virtue but the virtue of Mary.

Love is your gift to me, Mary, your gift of your virtue to be mine – and your Holy Spirit to be my saving and sanctifying grace.

I feel no satisfaction, at times, in praying to you, no satisfaction in fidelity. But that's all right, if only you will be my peace.

I have chosen to be an abject in the house of my Lady Mary...

O Mother and Spouse of the Creator, we cannot love you too much or surrender to you too absolutely. For you can only bring us Jesus and His Holy Spirit. God's delight has been to exalt you above every other creature. *The supreme created person is not an angel, nor even a man, but a women!* Here surely we have a solid foundation for a sublime theology of women's liberation.

If we would be honest in professing the equality of woman, there is no other way than by exalting to the greatest possible heights the "woman clothed with the sun." If we take seriously the teaching of Scripture and the Church on divinization by grace and glory, this will provide a fully adequate answer. For Mary has been divinized infinitely more than any other creature ever will be, by the gratuitous Gift of God to this supreme creature. God is our Father, Mary is our Mother. That is the absolute and ultimate truth. Always remembering that what God is by nature Mary is only by His gifts of grace and glory, the parallel is perfect: Mary, Beloved of the Father, Beloved of the Son, Beloved of the Holy Spirit – *Beloved of God!*

There is no danger of exalting Mary, for ultimately it is this very Lady herself who gives me clearly to understand that it is Jesus, infinitely more attractive than she, whom my love seeks. And it is this love of Christ that is "beyond the love of woman," but greater than, not less than the love of woman. And this we can learn, it seems to me, only through Mary.

It is true that when He was twelve years old you made a mistake in searching for the Boy Jesus in other places than the Temple, where He supposed you should know He would be. But considering that your study was a God-Man, I think you did pretty well. And 18 years later you understood Him perfectly. At Cana you said to the waiters, with utter confidence and assurance, "Do whatever He tells you."

At Cana, Mary, you took seriously the confidence Jesus had placed in His creature when He gave you the wondrous gift of freedom. You used it honestly.

You saw that your young hosts had run out of wine. So you very normally and simply said to this God-Man who was your Son, "They have no wine." When Jesus said to you, "What's that got to do with you and me, Woman? My hour has not yet come," you surely must have given Him a look that implied something like, "You can do something. For Your own Name's sake, do it." And He acted.

With all due reverence we can perfectly well say that there is a very great Mystery here, the Mystery of the dialectic of grace, by which it is God's will that no man, not even the God-Man, act alone, but only in company with and, in a certain sense, in obedience to a woman.

Immaculate Heart of Mary, our way to the God-Man, our life and hope under Him – *and* our truth and truthfulness! Lady, you do the same thing with us. We follow you, and you get us into situations where there is no alternative but to rise above logic to obedience.

No the Word is not enough. We need the Woman too – the Word Incarnate and the Woman clothed with the sun, the Word who is Jesus and the Woman who is Mary.

There is a wonderful story in the Book of Genesis. When Rachel married Jacob and went off with him, she took her household gods with her. When her father came angrily searching for them, she took the idols, "put them inside a camel cushion, and seated herself upon them. When Laban had rummaged through the rest of her tent without finding them, Rachel said to her father, 'Let not my lord feel offended that I cannot rise in your presence; a woman's period is upon me.' So, despite his search, he did not find his idols." (Genesis 31, 34-35)

Are we to say that Rachel is more gifted with ingenuity than Mary our Mother? God forbid. Mary, you are the

Woman who will smuggle us all into Heaven by hook or crook, if only we trust in you, and abandon ourselves to you, *absolutely*. We must do it your way, and then we will find that it really was God's way.

The way of love. O Mary, Most Sacred Lady, is it not true that every lady is sacred, and every woman a lady, as far as I am concerned, because for me she is you?

It *is* true.

Mary, you are my weakness. Be my only one.

Mother of God, bless all lovers. May they increase and multiply and save the world. "The world will be saved by beauty," wrote Dostoyevsky, true beauty, that looks out to you through the eyes from deep within the soul.

Sexual attraction must be dominated. It must be wholly and entirely channeled. And as St. Bernard says, Mary is the channel. How? As irresistibly lovely Lady Obedience, infinitely powerful because of the absolute union of her will with God's. She has learned obedience "through the things that she suffered," and learned it perfectly. Therefore she can teach it.

She is supremely innocent, truly and sublimely holy in a way that is both attractive to us sinners and susceptible of our poor, material, even "carnal" understanding. That is, Mary is beautiful. And because her beauty is absolutely true, devotion to her is completely safe. It was St. Paul who said, "Follow the way of love," and St. Therese of Lisieux added, "The way of love is a safe way."

O Mary, Queen of lovers, you are the lovely evening Star of the Sea, who when the way of love becomes stormy, make it safe for all of us.

Is not beauty love? Do we not call it "love-liness"? May not true beauty be defined as that which pertains to love? It is true that the lover has eyes only for his beloved. But he most certainly does have eyes for her.

O Mary, lead me to the truth about beauty and love, and to the love that lasts – forever.

"Union with the Bride, which is the Wisdom of God." Which is you, Mary. I am united with you "in the fear of the Lord."[30] And when this fear is perfect, love is perfect. "Man and woman must reconstruct, with great effort, the meaning of the disinterested mutual gift ... Is it possible to see in (biblical 'knowledge') some biblical equivalent of 'eros'? It is a question here of two conceptual spheres, of two languages: biblical and Platonic; only with great caution can they be used to interpret each other." [31]

"True possession in love ..."[32] O Mary, my Lady Obedience, it is you who possess me, my whole being and all my will. And if love may somehow be defined as the desire to be possessed by the beloved, I desire only to be more and more possessed by you. O Mary, I believe in you. Only because of you am I able to accept and realize that all the frustration of my life is simply building me, the only way possible – the good and best way – into what you want and wish me to be. Teach me this way of obedience.

It will be for me the way of fidelity. Woman is love, and man is fidelity or should be. But in our case, Mary, it is you who are all the virtue.

[30] The Ascent of Mount Carmel, St. John of the Cross

[31] Pope John Paul II, March 26, 1980

[32] Pope John Paul II

Yet love is fidelity. "Greater love than this no one has, than to lay down his life for his friends." O Mary, somehow I want to lay mine down for you, to live and die for the dogma of the Queen's virginity. St. Fidelis of Sigmaringen prayed throughout his religious life to die a martyr's death. And he did. O Mary, make my name "faithful" too by granting me the grace of such a fidelity.

I was dust mopping the dining room floor after supper this evening when it seemed to me you said to me, deep in my heart, "I love you." I thought of how the narrative of your apparitions at Guadalupe says that your words to Juan Diego "rejoiced him utterly." Then an hour or so later in church here it seemed to me that you said to me, "For you, I am the Lady of Peace."

When I feel frustrated, I speak to you, Mary, and you always listen. When there seems to be nothing I can grab hold of, and I still have to hold on, I search for you, Mary, and hold on to you. This is increasingly the case, and I feel it as the supreme blessing of my life – my utter need for you and your complete gift of yourself to me.

O Mary, you are for me "all that is true, all that is pure, all that is lovely, all that is gracious." I think about you – and the God of peace is with me. (Philippians 4, 8-9)

You are purity, Mary, as the most beautiful of God's creatures. I adore the wonderful Holy Spirit living in you more fully and perfectly than in any other created person. Yet in some mysterious way, my love for you is a true adoration of the Uncreated Beauty of Divine Grace which totally suffuses you. For though your person is distinct from the Person of the Holy Spirit, yet you two are absolutely – since your creation – inseparable.

O Mary, you are the Lady of the Rosary. If it please you, I would be the gentleman of the Rosary. For the Rosary is the only cure for the flight from beauty, which is ultimately the flight from love.

Lady of the Rosary, Scripture speaks of Moses as a man who held familiar converse with God "as friend speaks with friend." I feel that way with you, especially when I pray your Rosary. It was Moses too who saw your virginity, "burning yet unconsumed" in the figure of the Burning Bush. O Mary, your purity, your beauty, your love, all are one. I cast myself into your arms, and plunge myself into the searing flames – of the Burning Bush. And thus, just as St. Therese of Lisieux hoped for and attained true greatness in spite of or rather through her "littleness," so I firmly hope to attain to perfect love despite my overwhelming weakness, or rather by this very means: the weakness of love. For you are my weakness.

O Mary, the Holy Spirit made you fruitful with Jesus at the words of Gabriel, "You will conceive in your womb and bear a son." (Luke 1, 31) I will lovingly pray his words, "Hail! Mary! Full of grace ..." over and over, that they may make you fruitful with Jesus again and again, in us and through the whole world.

Taste and see that the Lady is good.

The Lady is my Shepherdess.

Humility before the Virgin, love for the Mother, obedience to the Queen and Lady.

Pope Paul VI is quoted as saying that Mary should not be thought of only as a Mother, but also as a Woman.

Devotion to her purity does not eliminate the reality of human nature, but sanctifies it. "Ask for a sign." And I asked, Lord, give me a sign, "high as the sky" (Isaiah 7, 11) And the sign appeared in the heavens, "a woman clothed with the sun," the Virgin with her child, Emmanuel – the Lady of Guadalupe, Mistress in a special way of all America.

Never underestimate the power of a woman clothed with the sun. Rather, surrender all attempts at estimates and just simply obey. And you will find in the end the joy of union.

It is true that Mary said to St. Bernadette at Lourdes that she did not promise her happiness in this life. But that does not mean that the Mother of God may not give her children in this world a little happiness if she wants to. No, she will *be* our very great happiness.

"Mary, the New Woman, stands at the side of Christ, the New Man, within whose mystery the mystery of man alone finds true light ... the Blessed Virgin Mary offers a calm vision and a reassuring word to modern man ... She shows forth the victory ... of joy and beauty ..."[33]

Be it so, then Lady Mary. Lead us obediently in the way of victory. Amen.

[33] Pope Paul VI, "Marialis Cultus," February 2, 1974

Epilogue

Mistress of Wisdom

Sedes sapientiae – Throne of wisdom....

0 Mary, eternally resplendent and "readily perceived by those who love" you, I have found you because I have sought you. (Wisdom 6, 12) Hurry! And make yourself known to me. Anticipate my desire. (6, 13) I shall watch for you at dawn, and "not be disappointed." (6, 14)

Scripture says that thinking about you Mary, is "the perfection of prudence." (6, 15) Here I am, keeping vigil for your sake. Scripture says I "shall quickly be free from care."

Why? How? Because you make your rounds, "seeking those worthy" of you – not that I am of myself, but you make me worthy – and "graciously appear" to them "with all solicitude." (6, 16)

First I desired you, then I loved you. Thus you captured me, and now I obey you. The future holds "incorruptibility," the gift of God's love through you, and closeness to Him and you in the Kingdom of Heaven. (6, 17-20)

O Mary, I honor you intensely, with that intense honor called hyper-dulia.

"I prayed," Mary, and you were given me, "I pleaded," and your spirit came to me. I preferred you – and still do and always will – "to scepter and throne." You are my whole riches, more priceless than any gem. All gold, in comparison with you, is like "a little sand," and silver is mud.

"Beyond health and comeliness" I loved you – and still do and always will, you who are even now my overwhelming reward. I chose to have you "rather than the light," because light yields to the darkness of night, but your splendor does not yield to anything. "All good things together came to me" in your company, for you are in your own person infinite riches for the poor. I have rejoiced in all things, Mary, for the reason that you are their Mother. (7, 7-12)

"Simply I learned" about you, "and ungrudgingly do I share," thou "unfailing treasure" to men, whom to gain is to "win the friendship of God," to whom the gifts you give them commend them. O Mary, you have taught me everything. (7, 13-22)

You are unique in intelligence and holiness among all creatures, the most perfect. Your perfection is infinitely manifold, embracing every perfection. You comprehend and rule the most subtle thoughts and movements of our minds and hearts and wills. You are immaculate. You possess all truth in the Beatific Vision of God in His Heaven. You are solid, faithful, dependable as a rock.

You are totally wholesome, safe, good and in love with the good, God. You are keen, and no flaw in my character escapes you. You are unhampered in your effectiveness by any drawback of fault or imperfection. You are kind. (7, 22-23)

Yet you are a firm disciplinarian, a determined teacher and a governor of my erring ways. You are secure both in your own virtue and power and in your control over me. You are ever tranquil, serene – Princess of Peace. You are all powerful, "Suppliant Omnipotence." And you see all. You know how sinful I am. Yet you see my basic desire for the good, feeble as it is, and because of it – even this your gift – you overlook my failures, even while making me repair them. (7, 23)

Your spirit, the spirit of the Virgin, is in all our spirits, in every spirit that is good. Yours is the spirit of our spirits. Yours is the true "spirit of the world," summing up all that is noblest and finest in the aspirations of men and women to serve one another. (7, 23)

O serene Virgin, O contemplative Lady, you are more active, more effective as an apostle than all the other apostles the world has ever known or ever will know. For your purity is humanly absolute and holds the key to the heart of every creature. Nothing, no one can resist your will. (7, 24)

For you are the atmosphere of God's power, and as such so powerful yourself that nothing can resist you. God's glory poured itself out in a Beauty beyond our comprehension when He created you. In a way, O glorious Mary, you are for us the glory of God itself. You are His pride, His boast, His masterpiece. Nothing sullied can enter you. Rather, all the sinful who approach you are transformed by nearness to you into innocent children who live thenceforth clean in your Mystical Womb, the Church. (7, 25)

Christ Jesus, your Son, is the Light, and you are His brightness, illumining, cleansing, rejoicing our hearts and souls and spirits. You are the spotless mirror, the perfect image of Jesus, just as – due proportion being kept – He Himself is "the image of the invisible God." (Col. 1, 15) You are "the image of His goodness." O Virgin of Guadalupe, thank you for your precious gift on the *tilma* of Juan Diego. (7, 26)

You are completely "one," whole, unfragmented by any lack of singleness of purpose or purity of intention or fullness of being. And this is the source of your perfect human participation in the power of God. You "can do all things." Your newness, your life, your vitality, your eternal youth and beauty and attractiveness, have the power to renew all things. You renew the world through the Church, and yes, in some mysterious way, even the Church through the world, wherever the values of purity, honor, loveliness, nobility are found among men, women and children. You are truly "The Eternal Virgin," and lovingly stealing into, and stealing away, human hearts from age to age, you transform countless multitudes into saints, multiplying the "friends of God." (7, 27)

For God loves only those who pass their lives in friendship with you who are purity and wisdom and love, whether they know you as the Virgin of Christian Revelation or not. (7, 28)

O Mary, you are lovelier than the shiny sun, when its overwhelming brightness dazzles the eyes and the heart as it lights up the gold and silver clouds in the pink and purple sky of a summer evening. You surpass the starry heavens of a clear winter night in the transcendent, soft and mystical sparkling of your holy beauty. (7, 28)

And this I love to repeat over and over again, most gracious Lady: *Compared to light itself, you take precedence.* "for that, indeed, night supplants, / but wickedness prevails not over" Mary. (7, 30)

Man must seek and follow the light. He must do right, seek virtue, obey the truth. But when he fails? And fail he will! *You* bring God's mercy and restoration to his soul. And not only this. More – when the wickedness of devils and men perverts the light, you lead us safe to the bosom of that Divine Wisdom who alone is the True Light, Jesus Christ our Lord, your own and only Son. "Lumen gentium *Christus* est." (*De Ecclesia*, Vatican Council II) You teach our hearts the holy conviction that the only light worth seeing is Jesus. And when even His Light seems to "go out" in the "dark night" of spiritual passivity, you remain with us, the created wisdom of God, and we find peace in spending the night with you, beautiful Lady Mary, who transform it into a night of love. (7, 29-30)

Indeed, powerful Lady, you reach with the infinite reach of your loving Heart from one end of God's cosmos to the other, with the irresistible might of your Mother's care, and as Queen of the Universe, moderate all things.

I loved and sought you from the time of my very boyhood days. Your beauty, Mary, it was your beauty that conquered me, for the Kingdom of Heaven, your truly heavenly beauty. Enraptured by its splendor, I finally surrendered utterly and threw myself into your arms, "O Immaculate Mother of Jesus and our Mother, Mary,"

(Pope Pius XII, 1954 Marian Year Prayer) and the flames of the Burning Bush set my heart on fire all over again with love, love, love. (8,2)

O most noble Queen, the immaculate beauty of your soul makes you the fit companion of God. "The LORD of all" fell in love with your loveliness and had to make you His Queen, if He as King of Truth were to be true to Himself and to you. (8, 3)

You are "instructress in the understanding of God." You are more than Newman's "model of the theologian." You teach love, which is the real theology. You teach the understanding of that Divine Being, that Transcendent Someone, who *is* Love. You obtain for us the gift of participation in His understanding, which is compassion and contemplation. (8, 4)

You are our wealth and our treasure, you the humble handmaid of the Lord, who made His very clothes, that wonderful "seamless tunic," woven in one piece throughout, that only a mistress of her art could have produced, for Jesus to wear to His glorification. You are a flowing fountain of virtues, "moderation and prudence, / justice and fortitude," which you teach by your splendid example, "and nothing in life is more useful for men than these." (8, 5-7)

You know all things in Christ. This is why I determined to seek your companionship, knowing that you "would be my counselor while all was well, / and my comfort in care and grief," "Though I be but a youth," you yourself would be my wisdom, my keen judgment. You would show me the way to immortality and conduct me along it. You would obtain it for me from God as a gift, who could never refuse you anything, or me this, for your sake. You would be my very virtue, and the memory I would leave behind forever among men. You would make me noble and courageous, with a share in your own nobility and courage. (8, 8-15)

But most wonderful of all, lovely Lady, "within my dwelling I should take my repose" beside you. O Mary! Wondrous gift of your mercy, your human love, your woman's heart! For what does it mean, beautiful Mary, this taking my repose beside you, except love, love, love, infinite love? O Immaculate Lady, I am yours, be with me! And to my astonishment, the Ever Virgin Mary grants my prayer. You come to me, Mary, to drift me gracefully, serenely into slumber beside you.

And what is it like? It is pure sweetness. There is real pleasure in friendship with you, Mary, good and wholesome pleasure. You are delightful to be with. Frequenting your society is true prudence.

Therefore, Lady, since I knew that I could wed you only by a gift of God, "I went to the LORD and ... / said with all my heart: / God of my fathers, LORD of mercy ..." give me Lady Mary, the Lady Wisdom, "the attendant at your throne," our Queen, to be my mystic Bride. "I am your servant / ... the child of your maidservant," (Psalm 116, 16) Mary's son. I am a weak man, "lacking in comprehension," poor in judgment. But even if I were perfect, I would still need this most perfect Mistress, Mary. For without her even the perfection of the perfect is worthless. For true perfection is only participation in hers, for she is the perfection of the Church. "Send her forth from your holy heavens," I prayed, "from your glorious throne." Grant me your Co-regent, to "be with me and work with me," that I may know and do what is pleasing to you. "For she ... / will guide me discreetly in my affairs," and the glory of her holiness will be my protection. "Thus my deeds will be acceptable." For who ever knew your counsel but by the gift of Mary. Truly, it is ever Mary who has taught men what is your pleasure. (8, 17 to 9, 18)

O Mary, you never "abandon the just man," but deliver him from sin. You go "down with him into the dungeon" of his suffering and comfort him when he seems held fast by unbreakable bonds – until finally you bring him to the royalty of perfect sanctity, perfect love, and grant him eternal life. (10, 13-14)

You provided Jesus and Joseph with the recompense of their carpentry labors in the nourishing meals you set before them at day's end and in the warm clothing you made for them to wear. Your woman's heart, your mother's heart, conducted them by its love along a wondrous road of domestic peace and happiness. That loving, feminine Heart of yours became "a shelter for them by day" from all the harshness of the world of struggle, and in the evenings and the nights the flame of its pure love kindled joy in their own hearts as you three would contemplate the starry heavens for a while before retiring to sleep. (10, 17)

When they grew thirsty at work of a hot day, they would call on you, and you would smile and bring them cool water. Indeed, your thoughtfulness was better than a ready-to-hand spring, for "You gave them abundant water in an unhoped-for way" – your smile was so wonderful that it was a joy for them to grow thirsty. (11, 4-7)

O Mary, Mistress of Wisdom, you willingly return the love of those who love you and search for you. You even anticipate our desires and are tireless in your longing to communicate yourself to men. (cf. Fr. Eugene H. Maly, Introduction to the Book of Wisdom, Pamphlet Bible Series)

The Lord has lavished you, Mary, on His friends. You inebriate men with your fruits. And just as you kept your holy house at Nazareth full of "choice foods" for Jesus and Joseph, so today you fill the Church likewise with nourishing good things for all your children. "Wisdom's garland is fear of the LORD ... " This garland is the Rosary, "the Garland of Roses." You shower down through it, Mary, "Knowledge and full understanding." You are our glory, the glory of the new Jerusalem. O Mary, help me to keep the commandments, that the Lord may bestow you upon me in all your fullness. (Sirach 1, 8-23)

O Mary, you instruct your children, and I am your child. Instruct me. You admonish those who seek you, and I seek you. Admonish me, till I am perfect in your love – He who loves you "loves life," and I have won your favor because I have sought you out. O Holy Spirit, help me, strengthen me, to hold "her fast," that she may be my glorious inheritance forever. O Lord, bless me, bless us all! (Sirach 4, 11-13)

O Mary, in serving you I serve God the Holy One. I love you, and that is why He loves me. I obey you. I hearken to you as best I can. Help me to do it always more and more perfectly, Mary, that I may dwell "in your inmost chambers." I trust you. Be mine. You have put me to the test, you have brought "Fear and dread" upon me, and tried me with your discipline. With your precepts you have put me to the proof. Now this heart is fully with you, fully yours. O Mary, make it so more and more, eternally. Reveal your secrets to me. Never let me fail you. Never abandon me. (4, 14-19)

And she answered me, "Even to the death fight for truth," and your Lady Mary "will battle for you." (4, 28)

O Mary, I embrace you! (6,18) 1 draw close to you. (6,19) You make me "labor but little," and you fill me with your fruits. (6, 20)

Is it true, Mary, that you are "not accessible to many"? (6, 23) O beautiful Lady, put these feet into your fetters, this neck under your yoke. These shoulders are all yours. Bind me to your service. With all my soul, I want to "draw close" to you, with all my strength I am trying to keep your ways. I have searched you out and discovered you, sought you and found you. *I have you*, and I will never let you go. Be my rest, my joy. I'm in love with these fetters, these bonds by which you keep me yours. You are my very clothing, O my Bride, O lovely Crown of my manhood. (6, 25-31)

O Mary, keep always before my heart's eye the remembrance of the pangs with which you are bringing me to birth. (7, 27)

My Lady, is not your power over me, in a certain sense, absolute? Are you not my true dignity? O Bride of Joseph, my heart is drawn to you irresistibly. Teach me to meditate and reflect on you, to ponder your ways in my heart, as you pondered the ways of Jesus, till I understand them.

I will "pursue [you] like a scout," and "lie in wait at [your] entry way," peeping through your windows, listening at your doors. I will encamp "by your home," next to its walls.

Make me your "welcome neighbor." I will be your loving little bird, and nest in the leafage of your branches. You will be my shelter from the heat, my home. (Sirach 14, 20-27)

Practice me, Mary, in the fear of the Lord, and in your law of love. Meet me like a Mother, embrace me "like a young bride," nourish me "with the bread of understanding" and quench my thirst by teaching me the truth. I, a sick man, sick with the sickness of sin, will lean on you, my faithful Lady, "and not fall." I will trust in you. You will be my glory and my eloquence, my joy, my gladness, my eternity. (Sirach 15, 2-6)

O Mary, you are enthroned high in the heavens, diffusing perfume like a rosebush. Bright and graceful Lady, to be with you is all delight. You are the fair Flower who bore eternally rich Fruit in the Son of God. I yearn for you, and you tell me to come to you and "be filled" with all the love you have to give. You are "sweeter than honey." You satisfy my hunger only to make me hunger yet more for you, my thirst only to make me thirst still more for your love. O Holy Spirit, help me, make me, always obey and serve her more perfectly.

O Mary, you are an unfathomable mystery, so deep are your thoughts, your counsels, so far beyond all other humans have you penetrated the mind of Christ. Make me a little "rivulet" flowing from the broad stream of your wisdom. (Sirach 24 passim)

O Mary, when I lose even the taste for food, it is you, the thought of you, that makes me want to eat again. Your "governed speech" and your "firm virtue" are inestimable blessings for me. By both you rule me gently but irresistibly. Your modesty, your chaste person are more radiantly beautiful than the sun rising in the heavens. Your virtue, which is all one with your beauty of face and graceful figure, is the very light of my eyes – your "shapely limbs and steady feet." (Sirach 26, 13-18)

You are the only girl I will ever have. Your woman's beauty lights up my face, "for it surpasses all else that charms the eye." And besides this, your words are so kind to me that truly my lot is far "beyond that of mortal men." You are my "richest treasure," more than a helpmate, "a steadying column." O Mary, "a man with no wife becomes a homeless wanderer." What would have happened to me if you had not taken pity on me, and in your mercy accepted me as yours? You are my only home – my honor, my reputation, my dignity, my very being, my all and my whole. (Sirach 36, 21-27)

O Mother of all the living, never let me leave your Mystical Womb, and grant that I may soon, very soon, come to the vision of you and your Divine Son in Paradise.

You are a treasure sweeter and better than any other wealth. Your love is more delightful than wine or music. Your voice is truer and sweeter than any melody. O supreme Flower, your charm surpasses all others. My prudent Guide, my loving Rescuer, your "sound judgment" teaches me the fear of God. You are for me all this glorious "paradise of blessings." (Sirach 40, 17-27)

Mother of God, make me a saint, and the one most dependent on you. From my youth I followed after you, a little boy enamored of a beautiful Lady. You were a rich Queen, the joy of my heart. I stuck to my quest and so attained to you at last. I strove to please you most perfectly, Mary, that you might never have to rebuff me. I was so in love that "I scrutinized my conduct ... and bewailed the sins of which I was not aware." I fixed on you my soul's desires. You cleansed me and showed yourself to me. You granted me the gift of understanding, the realization that you will never let me forsake you.

The vision of you stirred "my whole being." (Sirach 51, 21) You became my prized possession. "The Lord has granted me the request I made of Him."

O all you who need instruction, seek her, and she will be close to you. Seek earnestly, and you will infallibly find her. Look at me. "I labored but a little for her sake, and found great rest." Seek her, "and in his own time God will give you your reward." (Sirach 51, 13-30)

O Mary, whoever obeys you dwells secure, "in peace, without fear." (Proverbs 1, 33) "Long life" is in your right hand, in your left "riches and honor." You offer me my choice. And I respond by choosing only the love in your Heart. Your ways are "pleasant ways," and all your paths are peace. You are a "tree of life" to me. (Proverbs 3, 15-18)

Protect me, Mary, teach me to extol you, and to embrace you always "and in all ways." You are my life. (Proverbs 4, 6-13 passim) Do you alone give me water to drink, my Joy, my graceful Doe. May your love invigorate me always. (Proverbs 5, 15-22)

Mary, "You are my sister"! (7, 4)

Eternal Virgin, present in the mind of God in the beginning, when He first went about His work of creation, "His delight day by day, / playing before him all the while" helping Him as a little daughter helps her Father, teach me how to work and play always in the presence of Him and you, how to make my work play, and my play holy and good.

Make me happy in obedience to you. I mean make this obedience my happiness – to watch daily at your gates, waiting at your doorposts, knocking. For he who finds you "finds life" – and love! – "and wins favor" and salvation "from the LORD." (8, 30-35)

As a perfect Hostess, you have dressed your meat for your banquet, mixed your wine, spread your table. You have sent out your maidens, and through them you call out from the heights over the city of the world, "'Let whoever is simple turn in here; /... Come, eat of my food.'" (9, 2-5) What is this food, Mary? The Body and Blood of Christ, yes, which you give us by bringing Him into the world. This is the Bread and Wine of *meaning.* And for this Gift I will thank you forever – the Bread of Reality, the Wine of Beauty, the Gift of God.

O Mary, it is this the grace of Christ that constitutes your true beauty, and has won you all your honors, your gracefulness, your graciousness. I love you for it, and this makes my heavenly Father glad. (Proverbs 29, 3)

O Mary, you are priceless beyond all other pearls. In trusting my heart to you I have found "an unfailing prize." You bring me "good, and not evil," all the days of my life. Strong Lady, merciful, all loving, fearless, clothed with dignity, when I grow timid at the thought of the future, you inspirit me by laughing playfully at the "days to come." You speak to my heart the wisdom and "kindly counsel" of peace. O Mary, you are utterly wonderful. "Many are the women of proven worth," but you have surpassed them all. Others are charming but deceptive, and their beauty fleeting, but your charm, your beauty, is all penetrated with the grace of God – and heavenly. O Mary, He Himself is your reward. Make Him, along with you, mine as well. (Proverbs 31, 10-31)

Amen.

Postscript

The Gift of Joy

The Angel Gabriel is sent from God to a virgin engaged to a man named Joseph, and the virgin's name is Mary.

He says to her in her native Aramaic, "Peace! Most Highly Favored One! The Lord is with you."

Mary is afraid. God's ways with her had always been completely ordinary. She was afraid of the extraordinary. This young girl possessed the fear of the Lord in the fullest degree.

The angel goes on. "Of all women, happy you! You will conceive and bear a Son, whom you shall name Jesus, for He will save His people from their sins. He shall be great and shall rule in the House of Jacob forever."

Mary is astonished but reflective. "How shall this be?" Both she and Joseph have consecrated their virginity to God. What is God now saying? What is this that He wants? What is He asking of her? He alone is her Portion and her Part. How can motherhood be reconciled with this decision of hers which she has made only in obedient love for Him and which she knows He Himself inspired in her heart and in her will?

"How?" She does not doubt. Not for a moment does she doubt. Her question is not Zachary's, "How shall I *know*, this?" She *knows* it because God has spoken it, but she asks how it shall *be*.

And God is pleased to answer her. "The Holy Spirit will come upon you. The Power of the Most High will overshadow you. Therefore the Holy One to be born of you will be called the Son of God."

Mary has her answer. The Spirit of God! He is all powerful. He can do all things. He can do this thing. She realizes that she has become His Virgin Bride.

"Your kinswoman Elizabeth has conceived in her old age and is now in her sixth month. Nothing is impossible with God."

The words ring in Mary's mind. She has always known it. She knows it better than Gabriel who speaks it. Nothing is impossible with God. Nothing! Absolutely nothing! It will be the motto of her life. She will teach the world the meaning of faith, absolute and utter faith. She will stand by the Cross of a crucified God and remember that He said He would rise again, and in the universal darkness of this living death she will continue to believe more firmly and heroically than ever – that nothing is impossible with God.

And now her peace returns. Her calm. She is completely relieved of all fear and anxiety. Now there is left simply and only to obey. She is happy, and in her happiness she says, "I am the maidservant of the Lord. Let it be done to me as you say."

And with that the angel leaves her.

Let us not leave her. Let us remain with her, kneeling in the prayer of obedience and peace, with gratitude in our hearts for giving us this double miracle, of the Incarnation of the Word of God in the womb of a Virgin, and this tremendous little Mother, who from this moment forward bears in her Heart a solicitude for every creature. She is the Mother of God, of Angels and of Men, Universal Mother, this little Girl, in her humility and nothingness, the greatest of all God's creatures.

+

"Mary got up in a hurry and set out for the hill country of Judea." She did not remain long in that quiet of prayer. She must be up and doing. Elizabeth was six months along. She would have need of her. Mary's Heart beat faster at the thought.

But how did she travel? Alone? With Joseph? We do not know. She traveled. Let us be satisfied with this truth.

She arrived at the home of Elizabeth and Zachary in Ain-Karim in Judea. Elizabeth greets her with joy, and with the words of Gabriel, "Of all women, happy you," and adds some of her own, "and happy the Child of your womb." There is mystery here, the mystery of faith. Elizabeth knew because she believed and loved.

She loved Mary, with a deep and tender love. It is lovingly that she says to her, "And how have I deserved that the Mother of my Lord should come to me?"

She goes on, "At the sound of your greeting the child in my womb leapt for joy." There is a great and quiet joy in her love for Mary, and in Mary's for her.

And now it is time for Mary to speak: "My soul glorifies the Lord, my spirit rejoices in God my Savior, because He has regarded the lowliness of His maidservant. All generations shall call me blessed, for He who is mighty has done great things for me. Holy is His name. His mercy is from age to age on those who fear Him. He has shown might with His arm. He has scattered the proud in the conceit of their hearts. He has put down the mighty from their thrones and has exalted the lowly. He has filled the hungry with good things. The rich He has sent away empty-handed. He has given help to Israel His servant, mindful of His mercy, even as He spoke to our fathers, to Abraham and His posterity forever."

It was a blessed outpouring of her heart and soul. It was happiness quietly overflowing. It was gratitude to God, praise and love, humility and obedience.

"My soul glorifies the Lord." Yes, Mary, your transparent soul reflects all the glory of God. Its perfect splendor praises Him more than all the rest of creation, angels and men, stars and suns, put together. Your soul glorifies God, and gives Him a certain created but infinite glory. For there is not a blemish in you.

You are all fair, O Mary. O Immaculate Virgin, well may you find infinite joy in God, for you have never known anything but Him in all His universe of being.

He has looked lovingly on you, and found only truth. O Mary, make me true! I am eaten up by the falsehood of pride, a thing you never knew. And yet you can understand my misery.

O Mary, by your humility, deliver me. You are all powerful. Be my peace. I will thank you forever, Blessed

Lady. You are blessed forever, and the universe will sing your praises eternally. Blessed Mary! Blessed through all generations and blessed by all. He who is mighty has done incredible things for you. And you have cooperated. You have worked with Him harder than all other creatures. His name is holy, and He has likewise sanctified the name of Mary, and made it a sign of hope and solace for the wandering people of God.

You have brought us His mercy, Mary, you have shown us His power. We were hungry for His blessing, and He gave us not only Jesus to be our Savior, but you to be our Mother.

"He has given help to Israel." O Mary, how much we were in need of help. Mother of Perpetual Help, He has given us you, "mindful of His mercy," to be the ultimate sign of His infinite compassion as our Mother of Mercy. He is faithful to His promises, and we know that with you for our Mother we are sure someday to see the vision of God Himself in Jesus Christ, your Son.

"Mary stayed with Elizabeth about three months and then returned home." Your job was done, my Lady, your errand of love and mercy, and now your own time would soon be approaching, the fullness of time, and the Divine Mystery of Joy in Sorrow.

+

"A decree went out from Caesar Augustus...." The rulers of this world speak, the mighty decree, and the poor tremble and obey.

There is little justice in this world. That a pregnant

young wife should be forced to make such a journey as yours to Bethlehem is not right. What a great man Joseph! He does not go nearly mad with impotent anger. Quietly he obeys. Perhaps there was also a sword to pierce Joseph's soul, at the sufferings of His beloved Mary. O Lady, if only we could comprehend his love for you! But it is beyond the comprehension of either angels or men. What a man was Joseph! Joseph the silent one, the worker, obedient, absolutely and perfectly, incredibly obedient.

Joseph obeys. Together you journey to Bethlehem, the city of David, "because he was of the house and family of David."

Bethlehem, David's city, "House of Bread," the Bread that will feed the world.

But Bethlehem is crowded, and there is no room for this young couple – except in a stinky stable. And here the Son of God is born. "She brought forth her Firstborn Son, and wrapped Him round and laid Him in a manger..." And He transformed that smelly stable into a place for the King of Kings. It did not look any different – cold, drafty, dirty – and Mary and Joseph adapted to it and were happy. The God-Man brought with Him a joy that transformed that poor stable into a mystery of peace and prayer. He had come to save the world from itself. He came to Mary and Joseph, and they gave Him to us.

For we were present in the shepherds, "tending their flocks and keeping watch in the fields by night." Angels announced to them that Christ the Lord is born to be a sign to them as a Baby wrapped round and lying in a manger – a sign of poverty like theirs, a sign of blessedness for all the poor of all times and places, for us, who are poor in our need for Him.

"Let us go over and see this thing....and they found Mary and Joseph, and the Baby lying in manger."

For the first time Mary presented Him to the poor. The God of joy is the God of the poor. Only the poor know true joy, which is to have nothing but God. Jesus, my God, You said, "Ask, that your joy may be complete!" And yet, my God, I ask for You, not for Joy, knowing that all joy will come to me with You. You are my Joy.

Joseph had surely found a little straw to make a clean place for Mary and the Baby to rest. And it was fitting that the poor shepherds should not be overawed.

My God, by Your poverty You have given me confidence. You have convinced me of Your love. I am not afraid of a Baby resting in the straw of a poor stable. My heart is at peace.

Christmas is the Mystery of Peace. The same Star leads us all along the way of peace to find Mary and Joseph and the Child. Angels will be our companions, and we will be blessed in our poverty, enriched with the knowledge and love of the King of Kings.

Let us rejoice on this night. Let us be happy, for Christ is born. The Lord has come. God is with us, nevermore to leave us. The God of peace has come to be our Friend and Brother.

It is good, my God. Thank You for the Gift of Christmas! We are all Your children, and You give us this Solemnity as a special gift of love to the child in us. May we learn from You and from all the children of the world the simplicity and joy that will keep us truly blessed. Bless us children, children all, O Lord, bless our hearts, and teach us Your love. For all You ask is that we be Your children, grateful for Your unspeakable gift in Christ Jesus Our Lord. Amen.

+

"They took Him up to Jerusalem to present Him to the Lord, as it is written in the law of the Lord, 'Every firstborn male opening the womb shall be called holy to the Lord.'"

My God, I too was a firstborn male, and I have been consecrated to the Lord in a special way. I like to think that Mary offered me too to the Father as a victim for sacrifice.

Mary offered Jesus. In her the priesthood of the faithful found its highest expression. She offered her little Lamb to be sacrificed.

This is counted among the joyful mysteries, and rightly so, and yet the holy old man Simeon immediately appears to take the Child in his arms and announce that He is set for the rise and fall of many in Israel, for a Sign that will be contradicted, a Sign that will set men and women against one another, and that because of all this discord a sword would pierce the Mother's soul that the deepest thoughts, the real intentions of all these people, might rise to the surface and be made evident. It is the price of Motherhood. Motherhood is an exalted vocation. To be a good mother one must be a saint. After carrying them physically in her womb for months, a mother must carry her children spiritually in her heart for all the years of their lives, suffering their sins, being always there to guide or pray them back into the way of truth. And Mary is the Mother of us all. We are all her continually erring children. Christ has come to bring not peace but a sword, not unity but division. And it was Mary who paid the price of this in the suffering of her own soul. Paul and Barnabus have a sharp difference, Augustine and Jerome tangle in argument, all down the centuries the truth of Christianity sets good men and women against one another – for the sake of the most pure Jesus and His Mother. The pure truth. It is Fire! "I have come to hurl fire on the earth, and what will I have but that it should flame out!"

And yet it is the fire of love. Simeon had been promised by the Holy Spirit that he would not taste death until he had seen the Anointed of the Lord. Now Christ has come, and he holds the Baby in his arms and declares that now he is ready to end his life in peace, for his dream has come true.

And Anna, the elderly widow, who spent all her time in the Temple praying and fasting, now goes out to speak of Him to everyone.

There is joy for everyone but Mary and Joseph. Mary too had been joyful when she entered the Temple. But having offered her Son to the Father, it seems that now He will never be hers again. At the age of twelve He will leave her for three terrifying days. At the age of thirty He will leave her for three harrowing years. Then at His death, resurrection and ascension He will leave her behind in this world definitively until she finally rejoins

Him in Paradise.

She had surrendered once in Nazareth when Gabriel announced God's will to her. Now she surrenders again. It will be like this her whole life long, a way of numberless surrenders – to the will of God.

And Mary had much to surrender, infinitely more than we do. She had Him who was much more a part of her than He is of us. He was her Son, her Soul. She gave Him up and surrendered her whole being with Him.

He was the Firstborn, offered to the Lord, and the Lord would accept Him. But where he went Mary went. Where he was accepted Mary was accepted. In suffering, as formerly in what little joy the world had given them, they would be inseparable. The Mediator and the Mediatrix, the Redeemer and the Co-redemptress, the Son and the Mother, the Man and the Woman, the New Adam and the New Eve, repairing by their perfect obedience the original sin.

He was the Consolation of Israel, paid for by the desolation of His Mother. "Your own soul a sword shall pierce." O Mary, make my soul one with yours, that the same sword may unite us both. Mother of God, I would be true to you. Let me be wounded as you were – in the heart, in the soul. Amen.

+

"His parents used to go every year to Jerusalem for the feast of Passover...." Of course, they took the Baby with them, and then the Boy.

And now He is twelve years old.

The Passover has been celebrated. They are returning to Nazareth. In all the hustle and bustle and confusion, Mary thinks that Jesus is with Joseph, and Joseph thinks he is with Mary. The larger group sets out. Everything seems to be all right.

Then Mary and Joseph meet, and find that Jesus is not with either one of them. Still, they are not alarmed. "Thinking He was in the party," they continue their journey for a day. They look for Him "among their relatives and acquaintances." Little by little anxiety mounts as they fail to find Him. Where can He be? Finally, they conclude He is not in the party and return to Jerusalem to search for Him there.

By now Mary is frantic. He is only twelve years old. Jerusalem is a big city. She has the most perfect, the most sensitive of mothers' hearts. She is completely distressed. Joseph steadies her, reassures her. He has to be in the city. They will look and find Him. They will look until they find Him. They will find Him.

They search. They search all day long, all over the city. They do not find Him. By nightfall, Mary is on the verge of tears. Again Joseph reassures her. But she does not sleep.

The next morning, early, they begin again. All over the city they wander, asking here and there and everywhere for a twelve year old Boy. Hopes rise and fall, but mostly fall. No one has seen Him. Mary pleads with her Heart, but no one has seen Him. A second evening comes, and again Mary does not sleep, but spends the night weeping silently. Joseph holds her by the hand. They pray all through the dark hours.

Morning comes, and they are up even earlier than yesterday. They make their rounds – asking everywhere about a twelve year old Boy. They think of the Temple. They have not tried the Temple. They will try it. And there He is! All of a sudden! "Sitting in the midst of the doctors, listening to them and asking them questions." Jesus! His Mother pours out the Word in a rush of joy and happiness and relief. Jesus!

Then astonishment begins to set in, together with a kind of bewilderment. It is His Mother who speaks: "Son, why have You treated us like this? You see that your father and I have been searching for you in sorrow."

And Jesus answers. Why were you worried? Why did you have to search for me? "Didn't you know that I would have to be in my Father's House?"

Don't you know about me and my Father? But Mary and Joseph did not know – yet. "They did not grasp what He said to them." For Mary and Joseph it was pure mystery, a mystery on which Mary would long reflect. She looked at her Child, her little Boy, and said nothing.

But He was found, and she was at peace. They would return to Nazareth, and Jesus would go with them and be once again subject to them in all obedience, and His Mother would keep this mystery in her Heart, as she watched Him grow – "in wisdom and age and grace before God and men."

Truly He was a Mystery, this Boy, and yet He was her Child. She looked at Him, and her tears were no more, and her love for Him burst the bounds of the universe. Jesus! He was with her again.

But His Father. Yes, He was His Father's Son. She

would carry in her Heart for long years a wonder about this "Father" – and His Son. At the words of Simeon years ago, she had felt Him being taken from her. And now her surrender of Him was taken a step further. His Father! She was beginning now to surrender Him to this mysterious Father.

"My Father," Jesus called Him, and Mary reflected, and in faith said, "Yes."

Part Two

Poetry

My Ave Maria

I knelt to pray.
I began, “Hail, Mary.”
She answered, “Yes?”
I said, “Yes, what, most holy Mary?”
She said, “You hailed me?”
I cried, “Pardon me, Mary!
I didn’t mean to approach you the way I’d go after a taxi...
I was just saying ‘Hello!’ ”
She smiled.
I went on. “Full of grace.”
She said, “Yes, God has blessed me inestimably, uniquely,
with the gift of His grace.”
I agreed, “The Lord is with you.”
She said, “Indeed He is. And when you pray He is
with you too.”
I cried out with Elizabeth,
“Blessed are you among women,
and blessed is the Fruit of your womb, Jesus.”
She answered, “Truly, our Lord Jesus has blessed me
incomparably with the Gift of Himself,
but to a lesser extent He has likewise blessed the whole
world,”
and she bowed her head and prayed,
“and most blessed is He, our God.”
I too bowed my own head and begged,
“Holy Mary, Mother of God, pray for us sinners,
now and at the hour of our death.”
Her answer came smiling and sweet, loving and
reassuring –
“I certainly will, I certainly will, I most certainly will.

Be at peace."
"Amen," I concluded.
And she confirmed, "Yes, Amen, so be it."

The Prayer of Mary

Mary, I need to pray.
I need the the presence of God.
I have wandered away.
I need to come back to Him, and to you.
Gather my scattered forces, dear Lady, recollect my energies, and bring me back to myself
and to my God.
Make me pleasing to Him and to you.
Help me to begin all over again to seek Him in faith and to find Him in you.
Mary, bring me prayer.
Amen.

Pray to Mary

Mary leads to Jesus,
very gently,
very carefully,
very slowly –
but how very, very surely in the end.
Amen.

The Virgin Mary of Guadalupe

There's a picture of my Sweetheart
hangs upon my bedroom wall,
and I sit before it daily –
I just look at it, that's all.

Her hands are folded, and she prays
to the God within her Heart.
And to sit and just be with her,
that is all that is my part.

I will sit before her picture,
I will love her till I die.
I will sit there very quietly
with a teardrop in my eye.

The Gift of Purity

Mary, Virgin most pure, your gift is the gift of purity,
your way is the way of purity,
a pure heart, a pure mind –
pure love and loving purity,
silence and purity, the silence of love.
Amen.

The Prayer of Darkness

Silence is pure solitude
on a night in spring.
O Mary, Lady of the magenta evening,
I love you.

Do You Need a Knight, My Lady?

Do you need a knight, my Lady,
to slay a dragon or two?
I am ready to go into battle
for only the love of you.

O Mary, O lovely Damsel,
what distress can I free you from?
O put me in your service!
O supply me challenges some!

For I am the knight of my Lady,
my joy is to fight for her,
for you, O Queen of the Tournament,
for you, O blessed Mother.

The Pure Virgin

Mary is the Virgin Pure,
all pure, all purity,
more pure than purest crystal
in its purest symmetry.

Mary is the Virgin Pure,
the Miracle of Grace,
a purity so pure
she is the Purest of our race.

Mary is the Virgin Pure,
all pure, all purity.
O Mary, make me like you!
I'll say thanks eternally!

Lady Potter

Mary, when I think of you, my heart leaps for joy.
You are the Lady Potter
who mold me according to God's will.
Sweet Virgin Mary!
Amen.

My Shepherdess

Our Lady is my Shepherdess,
I have no one but she.
I am her little lamb,
and that I know I'll ever be.

She leads me in sweet pastures
where the grass is green and fair,
she comforts me with gifts of love,
she grants me gifts of prayer.

She is my Lady Shepherdess,
my Mother and my Queen.
She guards me and she watches me,
and on her help I lean.

Mary's Virginity

Not only perpetual, but also perfect,
absolute in the order of created persons.
Jesus' birth was miraculous:
"He did not diminish His Mother's virginal integrity,
but sanctified it."
Amen.

Exquisite Mary

I dreamt of the Virgin Mary,
and here's what I saw in my dream –
a Woman exquisitely lovely,
and courteous, and full of esteem

for me who am utterly nothing;
she gave me her hand and her smile.
And then I returned to my senses.
Yes, it only lasted awhile.

But I saw her – I'll never forget her,
the way she looked in my dream,
exquisitely lovely and giving her hand,
her courtesy and her esteem.

The Temple

Holy Mary, Mother of God,
make me a temple in which you will dwell,
where all your people
can find your love, your compassion and your peace.
Amen.

Maria

I'm only the "i" in "Maria" –
existence of my own I have none.
I'm only the "i" in "Maria"
till her work in me is done.

Lady Mary

Mary, Mother of God, where are you?
You are in my faith.
You are with me to strengthen me in faith,
to protect me,
to guide me in the way of prayer,
and every once in awhile to grant me an exquisite little joy.
O Mary, Mother of Jesus, I believe in you.
Lead me on to perfect love
and Paradise.
Amen.

Lady Purity

Mary, Mother of Mercy, what can I say to you?
How infinitely contemptible I am!
And how beautiful you are!
How lovely, how magnificent!
I am the disgusting beggar, and you the splendid Queen.
Lead me, O Mary, in the way of purity.
I am your poor little one.
Carry me in your arms.
Amen.

Mary

A very calm, quiet,
but warm and reassuring
presence.

Mary's

The man from the TV station told me
how to walk out of the plant store
holding a plant in front of me.
With camera in hand he said to me,
"I'm going to make you a star."
They've done one or two little five minute things on the
    Monastery.
But today, years later, as I was eating supper,
those words came back to me,
as if spoken to me by the Holy Spirit –
"I'm going to make you a star" –
not one of the Twelve Apostles,
who form the Crown of Mary "clothed with the sun,"
but perhaps a sparkling ring on her finger.
Yes! My Lady Mary!
Amen.

My Magnificat

My soul glorifies the Lady Mary,
my spirit is full of joy in her whom I love,
because she has looked favorably on the lowliness of her
    little slave.
She who is the powerful Queen of the Universe
has done great things for me.
Blessed be the holy name of Mary.
She is Mother of Mercy to all generations,
to those who call on her with trust and confidence and love.
Her glorious purity and beauty put the proud to confusion.
She turns the world upside down,

giving unspeakable joy to the little people.
She is a wise and loving Mother,
who fills the hungry with good things.
No one who comes to her does she reject.
She protects the whole Church – forever.
Amen.

Lady of the Spirit

O Mary, you are the woman clothed with the sun.
In Heaven now you are like an angel.
But are you an angel, Mary?
You are a messenger of God to me,
bringing me always His peace.
But are you all spirit, my Lady?
Perhaps, in a sense –
but somehow you also remain a Woman, a Mother,
Mother even of the Angels.
Lady of the Spirit, I think you are someone who constantly invite me,
and challenge me,
to be greater than I am, to grow.
And yet, dear Lady, what is growth?
It is growth in love, is it not?
O Mary, I need your humanness!
The created wonder that you are.
You are Purity, and I love you for it,
but you are pure *Wonder*!
And this I need in you, lest I wither away and die,
without desire, without hope, without love.
Lady of the Spirit, you are utterly lovely,

and there is not a blemish in you,
and I love you,
and I need you,
and I want you,
and I must have you,
and I surrender to you all over again,
and I will give you absolutely anything you want
if only you will let me be yours
and you will be mine
and take whatever I might not be able to relinquish of
myself.
O Mary, I offer you all!
Take me!
Suscipe me, Domina, secundum eloquium tuum, et vivam,
et non confundas me ab expectatione mea –
and give me yourself,
and your Jesus.
Amen.

The Mystery of Union

Sometimes I stop and wonder at how incredible it is that
there can be such a union of opposites,
utterly sinless Mary – and me.

My Lady

I don't have a TV set in my room,
and I don't want one.
I have a picture of the Virgin of Guadalupe.
I call it
Mariavision.

Queen of Paradise

Mary, Mother of God and our Mother,
I want to talk to you.
I would like to talk to you about Heaven.
St. Paul says, "We shall be always with the Lord."
What is it like, Mary? –
"...what eye has not seen, nor ear heard, nor has it entered
into the heart of man to conceive,
what God has prepared for those who love Him" –
for those who wait for Him.
I am waiting, Mary.
I know that God is wise,
that He will not take me to Heaven until the perfect
moment,
when I shall have been able to give Him the most possible
love.
If I continue to live in this world,
it is because God sees that it is good,
that I can grow more in grace and charity and love
and in all the virtues.
I thank You, my God, for Your wisdom and goodness.
By Your infinite power – I ask it once again –

and through the instrumentality of Mary, Your
    incomparably wonderful Mother,
make me a saint!
Mary, *you* make me a saint!
O Jesus, teach me Your love!
And Mary, be with me, now and at every moment,
and at the hour and moment of my death, my "transition,"
to the vision of His glory,
that I may pass from this world to the next
pleasing to God.
Amen.

Lady of Joy

Most Holy Mary,
what an inexhaustible source of joy you are for me!
What an everlasting fountain of youth and happiness!
Most beautiful Mary, I love you – make me true!
Have mercy on my weaknesses and imperfections and
    faults and failings and falls and sins,
on my selfishness and pride,
my anger and impatience,
my lack of charity and love –
on all of me, dear Lady, this whole bundle of miseries that
    I am.
But, Lady Mary, never let there be in me the slightest trace
    of malice.
Lead me in the way of utter sincerity and perfect innocence.
Make me and keep me always
your littlest child.
Amen.

Holy Mary of Guadalupe

O Mary, here I am, sitting in my room before your picture
in quiet simplicity.
It is a very quiet morning.
I could even doze off...
And what if I should doze off?
Am I not your child?
Is not my greatest need the need for humility?
O Mary, in simplicity and peace, I sit here in your presence.
All is calm, all is quiet.
Christmas is coming.
Today is the First Sunday of Advent.
Yesterday we sang at Vespers,
"Before me no god was formed, and after me there shall be none."
There is one God, and He is the God of Mary, the Son of Mary.
O Mary, teach me the profoundest adoration of "this Jesus,"
whom you bore in your womb for nine months,
whom you gave birth to in joy and bliss,
whom you nursed at your sacred breasts,
whom you held and fondled and caressed and clothed and fed,
whom you taught and reared,
whom you surrendered to the Father –
"this Jesus,"
with whom you died on Calvary even without dying,
and with whom you finally found eternal Paradise.
O Mary, my Mother, lead me there too,
with all my family and friends,
the whole human race,

to be with you and Him forever
in undying love.
Amen.

Mary, Teach Me!

Lady in rose and turquoise,
Lady of the raven hair,
Lady of peace and purity,
Lady! Hear my prayer!

Make me one with you, Mary,
in virtue forevermore.
Make me cling to you, Mary,
and with you Jesus adore.

Make me true to Him, Mary,
with love infinite and whole.
Give me no rest, my sweet Lady,
until I've attained this goal.

Teach me His love, Lady Mary,
Jesus, Your Son and our God,
teach me humility, Mary,
humble me down to the sod.

Grant that I never know anything
save but the love of Christ,
and die with Him who for love of me
at silver pieces was priced.

The Presence of Mary

O Mary, Mother of God, I believe in you.
I know you are with me, by faith I know it.
And I believe in Heaven.
I know in faith and hope that someday you will come with
Jesus
to take me to yourself,
and I shall be happy with the Lord and with you forever.
The thought gives me great joy.
But that time is not yet.
Now is the time of waiting and hoping, praying and
suffering.
However, love is the next best thing to Paradise,
and even now I can love.
I can love you, my Lady, and I do.
You are with me.
Your presence is with me.
I do not exactly feel it,
but I know in faith that you are here with me as I write.
The writing helps me to make acts of faith in your
presence,
so that I almost feel it.
You give me peace and the assurance that all is well,
even though I am a sinner, a sinful man.
I do not love my sins.
I love you, Mary.
It is good to be still with you in the evening like this
here in my room.
It is almost a kind of foretaste of Heaven.
Mary! You seem too good to be true!
And yet I know that it is the truth that you are with me

and waiting for me ahead in Paradise.
O my Lady, what can I say?
I cannot hurry things.
The wisdom of God says that I am not yet "done."
I am not yet ready for Heaven.
So be it, Mary.
I am happy this evening simply thinking about you.
How wonderful you are, Mary!
How wonderful the Creator of such a being as you!
But I must remain quiet,
or I will lose the sense of your presence.
It is an exquisitely delicate thing.
It cannot last long.
But I thank you, my Lady, for this grace of this evening,
solitude with you in pure faith.
When I began to write I was lonely and alone.
Now I am in your presence.
O Mary, do not leave me alone.
I cannot bear it.
I would return to creatures.
And my heart would agonize when it cannot have them.
Yet they are good.
But you, my Lady Mary, my Lady Obedience, are better.
Must I stop now, Mary?
I cannot bear to.
Your silence is a sweet and pure caress.
O Mary! Stay with me, remain with me,
throughout the night and always,
my Mother, my Beloved One,
my Sweet and Wondrous Everything.
Amen.

Queen of Heaven

O Mary, Queen of Heaven, Queen of Paradise,
I want to be with you.
I wait in hope, and I pray, and my heart aches.
You do not promise me happiness in this life,
and I suffer.
You are my hope, with Jesus.
You are my consolation.
Sometimes, in fact, the bitterness of life becomes utterly
sweet, dear Mary, because of you.
My Lady, come!
Come take me home to you!
Perhaps the reason that I go on living in this world
is that I do not powerfully enough desire Heaven.
O Mary, you know I desire it.
You know I long for it.
My Lady, I want to go Home!
Come take me!
Mary, live in my heart.
Be with me, remain with me,
these last days and weeks and months.
Be my peace, my sweetness, my joy, my solace.
I have no rest except in your presence in prayer.
I hope in your goodness,
your infinite mercy, compassion, understanding, love.
O Mary, have I loved you?
I am a sinner.
But mixed up in all my sinfulness,
and deeper down than any of it,
is my love for you and for the Heart of Jesus.
I will simply pray, and think no more about anything.

I do not have to explain to you.
I cannot explain.
Prayer sums up the whole mystery
and unites me to you in quietness and confidence.
O Mary, this is a prayer, this my writing,
along with the Rosary.
I want to live forever, pray forever, remain forever in your presence.
Never leave me, Lady,
from this present moment until the moment of my death
and for all Eternity.
Stay with me, Mary.
Keep my heart present to yours forever.
Amen.

Thank You

Mary, Mother of God, Blessed Lady,
my life is becoming an adventure,
as I move forward along the way of survival moment by moment.
I go along in faith, unable to pray.
I wait.
Now I have a little peace,
and I thank you for it.
O Mary! Thank you for everything!
Thank you for the gift of suffering
and the gift of your love.
Amen.

Fidelity

We are free.
That is the awful truth.
We have free will.
We have to have it in order to love.
God has given it to us in order that we might love.
But what this also means is that we can choose not to love.
Judas betrayed Jesus Christ.
We are able to do the same thing.
That is the truth.
But there is another truth,
a deeper truth,
a secret truth.
The secret of fidelity to Jesus is Mary, His Mother.
"Whoever finds me finds life,
and wins salvation from the Lord."
Mary is, in the words of the Second Vatican Council, the
 "sign of sure hope..."
Whoever finds Mary, the Mother of God, finds fidelity to
 Jesus Christ.
It is a Mystery.
It is a tremendous Mystery.
It is the Mystery of the Mother.
But I dare to say it:
Whoever finds Mary finds permanent fidelity to Jesus.
I dare to say it:
If we go to her, she will not let us betray Him.
If we pray to her,
if we trust in her,
if we give ourselves to her as to His Mother and ours,
she somehow –

most lovingly and most mercifully –
captivates our will,
so that we are simply unable to betray her Son.
The truth remains that we work out our salvation in fear
and trembling.
But in finding Mary
we also find the truth of love and fidelity and confidence
and security and peace.
The Mother of God confirms us in peace,
as she confirms us in final fidelity.
There will be struggles, many and great.
There will be trials, many and subtle.
There may be failures, smaller or larger.
But there will be substantial, final fidelity.
Can one count the number of betrayals in the world today,
in the Church today,
of Jesus and His Truth,
the Truth that He is?
And yet for us there is peace.
"A thousand shall fall at your side,
ten thousand at your right side."
Near the child of Mary disaster shall not come.
Devotion to Mary, as the Church teaches, is a "sign of
salvation,"
a sign of love for "this Jesus,"
a sign of fidelity to His Truth.
Yes, there is a secret,
and it is Mary, the Ever Virgin Mother of God.

My Easy Way

I am not a strong man.
I am not a virtuous man.
Yet I want to be a saint, and as great a saint as possible.
Should I give up this desire?
Obviously, no.
Then it must be somehow possible for me to become a great saint
in spite of my sinful weakness.
For with God all things are possible.
What, then, can be for me the secret of spiritual success?
St. Therese of Lisieux rejoiced
when she found her completely "new" way,
her "little" way of spiritual childhood.
Well, this is great.
But she also speaks of "always choosing the most perfect path," etc., etc., etc.
I don't seem to be able to do that.
Yet she has inspired me with the great and intense desire
to become the saint that I know God wants me to be.
I am much weaker than she was.
What I need –
and perhaps many other people too –
is precisely an *easy* way.
St. Maximilian Kolbe said that religious who are devoted to Mary, the Mother of God,
find their vocation "easier" than others who do not have this devotion,
or have it to the same extent.
O Virgin Mary, Loveliest of women –
as the Holy Spirit calls you in the Song of Songs –

surely your pure Heart, your immaculate Heart,
will be for me the "easy" way to great sanctity
that I need absolutely.
O Mary, I have no other hope.
I place all my trust, absolute trust, in you,
to bring me the fullness of the Holy Spirit
and lead me to Jesus.
O Most Blessed Mary, Queen of Fair Love, make me holy
like you.
O Mary, *be* for me the fullness of the wonderful Holy Spirit.
Sanctity is a mystery, a gift of grace.
And you, my Lady Mary, are the secret.
With you all things are possible.
Thank you, my Lady.
Amen.

Mary Most Holy

The great Mother of God
stood beneath the Cross of Christ
and died a thousand deaths,
endured a thousand martyrdoms,
with Him.
O Mary, I want to experience one of them.
If more were possible, I would ask for more.
You are nothing in comparison with God,
and I am nothing in comparison with you.
Amen.

Prayer

O Mary, Virgin of Guadalupe, I sit here before your picture in my cell.
You are with me – I know it by faith.
I do not experience your presence now in quite the same way as I used to.
It seems that my faith is being refined.
Yet you are the same wonderful Lady, the same Queen of my heart.
O Mary, shall I say once again that I love you?
You are with me, and that is enough.
Silence is enough, faith is enough.
Faith is the only prayer I have anymore.
It is the only prayer I can pray today.
But it is enough.
You give me your word that "all will be very much well."
You give me your Word, Jesus.
I cannot see, I cannot feel, but my hope is very great.
I hope for perfect charity.
I want to love – to love mightily, to love eternally, to love divinely.
The world would consider me a fool to nurture in my heart so great a hope.
After all, who am I?
I am nobody, I am nothing.
Ah, but I am the child of Mary.
My heart belongs to the Queen of Heaven and Earth, the Queen of the Whole Universe,
and hers belongs to me.
"I am her fool a hundred thousand ways,"
in my obscurity – unknown, unsuccessful.

Why do I hope?
Because of the Promise of God, because I love.
But my ardent love is being transformed now more and more into a quiet, stable hope.
My hope is no longer of this world.
My hope is of Heaven.
I live now only for a better world.
O Mary, you are for me the sign of that better World,
you who are Queen of Heaven.
I cannot imagine it.
It is the Kingdom of the Spirit.
I only wait in faith.
Certainly I am a failure.
A certain element in society might say that I am not an absolute failure.
I have found a certain balance in life, a certain reasonable peace, a certain measurable success.
But the world cannot really see.
In this world I have found nothing.
No, my success is in my heart.
My success is entirely within, in my surrender, in my submission.
O Mary, my Lady Love, you are my success,
you who give me your Word, Jesus,
that He will somehow use my infinitely less than nothingness
to further His plan of salvation for the whole human race.
My success is my faith.
My hope is a great and holy thing.
O Mary, you bring me the Holy Spirit in all His fullness.
You bring me truth and peace.

What is my work now, Lady Mary, in this world?
Only to surrender and submit ever more and more.
Only to be mystically annihilated ever more and more before "this Jesus,"
who must increase as I decrease.
Only to wait patiently, only to suffer, only to love.
It seems that I am no longer really a part of this world.
My love for people has become my hope of Paradise.
All is converging on the End.
I hope that I will draw many, many, many people with me
to the Gates of Heaven.
Hope is my prayer, faith is my hope.
Love now consists for me only in the patience of one who waits.
The Kingdom of our God and of His Christ is coming.
Let there be peace.
Let there be complete surrender and perfect submission to the will of God,
and to His Mother, Mary.
Amen.

The Virgin Birth

"There are fifteen known cases of human parthenogenesis" – virginal conceptions.
But there has been only one Virgin birth,
"natura mirante" at the miracle,
the hymen intact.

Mary, My Lady Obedience

Mary said to the Angel Gabriel,
"I am the maidservant of the Lord.
Let it be done to me as you say."
She is obedience personified, obedience to the truth that is Jesus.
Hers is the spousal obedience of the Bride, the Church.
She stood at the foot of the Cross and wept.
I would stand with you, my Lady,
as your knight, in what St. Benedict calls,
"the shining armor of obedience."
Obedience! Obedience! Obedience! Mary, my Lady Obedience!
Amen.

Truth

In this sinful society in which we live,
the Way of Mary
is not only for us the way of wisdom,
but the only way even of truth itself.

Mystery

"The Trinity among Christians" –
the Blessed Virgin Mary, the Pope and celibacy.

O Mary!

O Mary,
you are like a summer evening
when the setting sun makes pink clouds in the pale blue sky.
You are like the peace and silence of a summer evening,
when only the birds are chirping off and on
and day is spent.
Sweet Lady,
sweet summer Eve,
I know a lady who communes with flowers.
O Mary,
fair evening Flower,
teach me communion with you.
Amen.

Prayer

O Mary, wonderful Mother of God, I am here once more with a problem.
I feel great bitterness in my heart, I am suffering a very bitter thing.
It is my own fault – for straying from you.
O Mary, I desire a pure heart with my whole being,
and I suppose this bitterness is the price I must pay.
I desire you, Mary, my only Lady – I want to have no one but you.
But why should this hurt, Mary?
It's a beautiful evening, my Lady.
The sky is clear, delicate pale blue, with wisps of white cloud streaked all across it.

There is a hint of pink, especially near the horizon.
All this blue, white and pink is reflected in the water of the lake.
It is exquisitely lovely –
like you, Mary,
Queen of the pale blue sky.
It's quiet.
Only a few birds are chirping here and there.
But I'm not enough of a naturalist to recognize any of them.
There are two or three jets overhead, but far distant, barely audible.
The Canadian geese at the shore of the lake seem to be at rest for the evening.
Oh yes, I just recognized a couple of Bob Whites.
Here comes something like a Piper Cub overhead.
The clouds look like "Angel's Hair."
All is at peace.
And, my dear Lady, sitting here with you on this bench,
I too am beginning to feel at peace.
The world is too beautiful for much bitterness to survive in it for very long.
You are too beautiful, Mary –
Lady of the Summer Skies.
O Mary, I am at peace!
Beautiful Mother, it is your doing.
It is purely the effect of your presence –
in all these beauties,
in all this silence, this quiet.
My Lady, I love you.
Amen.

Cana

Where the waters blushed
at the power of the beauty
of Mary,
and reddened into pure wine.

The Good Girl

The good girl lived in Nazareth
twenty centuries ago,
and she loved the good with passion
and from head to little toe.

Then one day she went to Heaven,
by the grace of God, you know,
was assumed there by a special gift,
to be near her good St. Joe.

Now she speaks to us of goodness
from her place in Paradise.
Let us listen to her words of this,
for they are without price:

"The image of God's goodness I,
the wisdom of His grace,
the love of His most sacred Heart,
the beauty of His Face.

"The mercy of His justice I,
the weakness of His strength,
the gift of His compassion I
throughout the world's broad length.

"His all-embracing care am I,

His Mother and His Queen,
His Providence and Prayer am I,
and everywhere I'm seen.

"I penetrate society,
a spirit feminine.
I pass with all propriety
into the hearts of men.

"I have compassion on the poor,
the erring and the stray.
I bring them back to Heaven's door,
I bring them back alway.

"I am the good girl at her prayer,
I am the faithful one.
And I am she who suffers,
for I'm also everyone."

The Quiet Pearl

She was quiet, she was gentle,
was this pretty smiling girl.
She was peace and she was goodness,
was this matchless human pearl.

She was rose and she was lily,
she was flower perfumed rare.
She was miracle and marvelous
and all beyond compare.

For her Heart beat for the sparrow
and the little things that crawl,
and it beat for little you and me,
and for us most of all.

For it beat for Him who for her love
became a Baby small –
and it beat for Him with ardor
and with gift beyond recall.

For He it was who'd made her
such a quiet, lovely girl,
and He wooed her for the quiet
of her very hair's least curl.

Yes, He wooed her in the quiet
of a Heart that knew no sin,
and He won her there in silence
and He wed her there within.

And she kept Him in her heartbeat
till she gave Him birth to men.
And He died to save her silence
from the world's unsacred din.

Then He took her to His Heaven
where the quiet one is Queen.
And her smile remains as quiet there
as 'twas of yestere'en.

Maria, Rosa Mystica

My love's a Flower fair,
  a Flower rare.
My love's a Flower red,
  a brilliant red.
My love's a flaming Rose –
  from head to toes!

Regina Mundi,
Queen of Troopers

The Lady I'm in love with
is a Lady all the way.
Yet she has no scorn for workers
and cares not what people say.

She has blessed the loud air hammer
with her blessed Lady hand.
She has blessed the man who wields it,
she has blessed that whole hard band.

She has blessed the tough truck driver,
she has blessed his heavy load,
she has blessed the miles he travels,
she has blessed his long loud road.

She has blessed the girder worker
who walks steel up in the sky.
She has kept his heart in her heart,
that he might not fall and die

She has blessed the oil driller
and the mighty rig he tends.
She has blessed the salvage worker,
saved him from the deep sea bends.

She has blessed the sweating farmer
and the heavy work he does.
She has blessed the migrant women,
suff'ring, picking cotton fuzz.

She has blessed the secretary,
ragged at the end of day.
She has blessed the nurse and nurse's aid

and works with them alway.

She has blessed the men and women
who toil o'er the world each day,
o'er the noisy, fast, ferocious world –
and the children as they play.

And she's blessed the children that don't play,
the children of the streets.
Yes, it's these that she's blessed most of all
as she meets them on her beats.

She's a Trooper, is this Lady,
she's out there with everyone,
and she'll be there until doomsday,
and she'll get the world's job done.

She is suff'ring with the wounded,
she is dying with the slain,
she is Queen of this world truly,
truly as it toils in pain.

Beautiful Mary

O Mary,
I see your face in every pretty girl's.
I see your glory in the light of early dawn,
your beauty in the evening sky,
your loveliness in the stars of deepest night.
I find your dress in every flower,
the wonder of your faith in every praying child's.
You are ravishing in the rainbow, magnificent in the
mountains.

You sparkle in the sunlight on a summer lake
and speak to me in the silence of the snow.
O lovely Lady,
the world is beautiful because you are beauty,
the universe is splendid because you are splendor,
time is graced and eternity will be glorious
because you are the grace and glory of God.
Amen.

The Glory of Mary

Once there was a sinful sinner
who was steeped, all steeped in sin.
Yet he hated sin with hatred
but the battle could not win.

He was bound, it seemed, to go on sinning
till the day he died.
And he felt that every time he prayed
he did not pray but lied.

Life went on like this with him for years,
for years, years of despair,
until one day he lifted eyes
tear-filled to the Virgin Fair.

He prayed, "O Mary, can you help me,
ev'n one such as I?"
And then he broke down there before her
and began to cry.

How long he knelt he didn't know,
the tears how long they came
he didn't care, for he was sunk

in woe and sin and shame.

But finally his strength was spent,
the wellsprings of his eyes
were dry, and ev'n his heart was dry,
as soul with desert vies.

Then Mary smiled and touched him,
and she reached down with her hair,
and wiped that tear-stained face of his
with the Glory of th' All Fair.

And the sinful sinner felt such bliss
that he died right then and there –
yes, he died for love of Mary,
for the love of the All Fair.

Still, folks thought that he was living,
for he still seemed to walk where
he had always walked in former days
before that day of prayer.

But he wasn't – he had died for sure,
and he lived in Heaven now,
in the memory of that moment
when the Queen's hair touched his brow.

Is Not His Mother Called Mary?

Lady of Sorrows, O Bitter One,
who stood beneath the Cross
and drank the cup of suffering,
bitterest awful loss,

O Longed for Child of the Universe,

who gave the world its Christ,
and gave the Father His only Son,
at silver pieces priced,

O Mary, O Mother of All Mankind,
I wish to stand with you.
O Bitter One there at the foot of the Cross,
some bitterness grant me too.

O Mary, I wish to suffer with you.
Oh, let me prove to thee
that Motherhood, though it hurt very much,
may not all bitterness be.

The Laboring Lily

She washed pots and pans and swept the house and
changed God's diapers too.
She bore cheerily from the water well
jars heavy not times few.

She spun wool and sewed good garments
for her Son and husband great.
She worked hard as all the poor must work,
and long, and sometimes late.

She cooked meals and made them tasty,
building up from scratch good fare –
and it's not always so easy
when the cupboard's somewhat bare.

But she labored hardest at the prayer
that brought Christ to us men.
That was pure labor laborious

when she helped God victory win.

For she labored hardest at the Cross,
when from the side of Christ
was the Church born, as she Mothered both –
and Bride and Bridegroom spliced.

The Ballad of Lady Obedience

Gather 'round, little children, one and all,
and I'll tell you a tale that's far from tall –
how I courted and wooed her and paid her calls,
but still seemed to meet with nothing but falls –
    of the winning of Lady Obedience.

How I prayed, how I sighed, how I wept hot tears,
how I nearly despaired from all my fears,
how I cried and cried and cried and cried,
how I felt there was no one at all on my side –
    oh, the courting of Lady Obedience!

How I opened the Bible and looked inside,
how I read, "She'll embrace you like a young bride,"
how she finally said to me, "You silly boy,
I've only been building your hope and your joy
    of the wedding of Lady Obedience."

How I started to hope and began to long,
with a yearning so strong, so strong, so strong,
that I started to thirst and began to groan,
to moan and moan and moan and moan
    for the wedding of Lady Obedience!

Oh, her promise to me was so much sweeter
than honey! I queried where I should meet her.

She said, "You silly, meet me in church."
And that in a way was the end of my search
and the wedding of Lady Obedience.

Yes, I met her in church on the eighth of September.
'Twas a bright sunny day I'll forever remember.
Now I say with the prophet what he said of his doe,
"I have found her my soul loves – I won't let her go!"
I am wedded to Lady Obedience.

So wherever you roam or wherever you go,
be sure that you're not too awfully slow
to tell the story of all my woe –
of my courtin' and wooin' and bendin' so low
for the winning of Lady Obedience.

Will I meet her in church on the twelfth of December
this time, when death comes, my limbs somewhat less limber?
I don't know, but I know that death won't come as dreaded –
it will come as the Virgin, Lady Mary, I wedded
when I wedded my Lady Obedience.

O Mother Mary

Mother Mary, I'm in love with you,
in love with your folded hands,
in love with the fall of your raven hair,
with the way my Sweetheart stands.

Mother Mary, I'm in love with your eyes
that pray so silently,

in love with the gown all of rose you wear
and the turquoise that veils thee.

I'm in love with the sash about thy waist
and the Cross in the brooch at thy neck.
I'm in love with the beauty of thy fair face
and in love beyond all reck.

I'm in love with thy loveliness utter quite,
with the peace thy presence brings.
I'm in love with the prayer thy Heart doth make
with a love my own heart sings.

I'm in love with love personified
in a woman so all fair
that the angels look the other way,
their hearts blindness to spare.

But I do not look the other way,
O Glorious Lady mine –
In confidence serene, sublime,
mine eyes into thine shine.

And there I see all mystery
of love and love and love.
I see that beauty's naught but love –
just love, love, love, love, love.

I contemplate thy figure
and the moon on which you stand,
the sun that clothes thee, stars that crown thee,
all that brilliant band.

I gaze upon the universe
surrounding thy sweet form,

and I see why God made nebulae
in numbers past all norm.

I love you, Mary, Mother mine,
your own obedient Will.
I'll love you for forevermore
and then I'll love you still.

I'll live for you and die for you
upon a Cross of love.
And then I'll rest in the arms of you
forever, in Heaven above.

The Obedience of Faith

Life is a party at which we play games,
and "Blind Man's Buff" is one of their names,
when Mary the Virgin leads blindfolded me
through the darkness of faith to Eternity.

She smiles, and I feel her sweet hand in my own,
but naught can I see save the faith she has sown
in this heart that does follow wherever she leads.
"Oh, have mercy!"s the prayer that that heart ever pleads.

Prayer

Mary, dearest Lady, I need to talk to you again.
I have a problem.
I think the problem is me.
And I think the solution is you.
So much of the time it is your beauty and your love,
your kindness, your presence, your immaculate Heart,

that are the solution to all my problems.
O Mary, I need your love!
I belong to you.
I do not belong to myself.
Therefore from this moment I cease to be my own problem.
If I am a problem, I am your problem, for all that I am is yours.
Mary, what is the problem?
That my heart has been away from you.
For you are never away from me.
It is the problem of faith.
I believe in you, Mary.
You said to St. Bernadette that you did not promise her happiness in this life.
But, Mary, is it not the whole purpose and meaning of prayer
to unite me to you?
And if I am united to you, how can I be unhappy?
It is a mystery.
The mystery of reality is a mystery of suffering.
But union with you means something, does it not?
Does it not mean peace, my Lady?
And how can I have peace unless I can be confident and sure
that I am loving you infinitely, perfectly,
with my whole heart and my whole soul?
My Lady, I long for your presence.
I long for Paradise.
I cannot rest in the unhappiness of this world.
I cannot rest in anything but a foretaste of the possession of you in vision.
I can rest in true peace,

but only union with you can give me this true peace.
Mary, I am a sinner, as you know better than I.
It seems that the only virtue I have is the virtue of desire
for you, the desire to please you.
But this is an infinite desire!
Come to me, Mary.
Speak to my heart.
Grant me the peace that I do not deserve,
by granting me an increase of your love –
effective love, real love, for you.
My Lady, teach me to pray.
Be with me, now and always,
that I may live always in your presence
and die in your embrace.
Amen.

Prayer

Mary, my Lady, I want to talk to you.
It is a simple desire of my heart.
I am a sinner, and I need you.
I need your truth, I need Jesus.
But I need you too.
I need a Mother, I need a Bride.
Life is hard, and often quite sad.
O Mary, Cause of Our Joy, how we need you to bring us
happiness.
It is true that we are living for a better world,
but we cannot live without some happiness in this one.
Mary, our true happiness!
Thank you, my Lady, for the gift of your truth.

I will bless you for it in good times and bad.
But I thank you also for being the joy of my heart,
without which I could not live.
It would not be good for me to have joy all the time.
I cannot even have peace all the time.
But some joy and some peace are an honest need of my
soul.
O Mary, be that true joy and that true peace!
Cause of Our Joy, Queen of Peace, be with me as I write
these lines,
and in all my prayer –
in all my daily life.
Be with me when I rise from sleep in the morning,
when I go to Mass and eat and work,
when I pray and read and eat again.
Be with me when I drop off to sleep in the evening,
and be with me through the night.
Beautiful Mother, beautiful Queen, I would dream of you,
that my whole life may be only one long uninterrupted song
of love
to you, my Lady Fair,
Mary of the raven hair.
Amen.

Mary's Victim

The wonderful "Little Flower," St. Therese of Lisieux,
tells of how she heard of people offering themselves to God
as victims of His justice.
She says she admired this,
but was not personally attracted to it.

Rather she felt inspired to offer herself to Him
as the victim of His merciful love.
In reflecting on all this,
something further occurred to me.
God and Mary were partners in our Redemption,
at least in a certain but very real sense.
Mary "co–redeemed" us in subordination to the redeeming work
of the one Divine Mediator, the God-Man, Jesus.
So I asked myself –
"Why should not Blessed and Beautiful Mary also have a victim of love?"
And I could think of no reason against it.
So I offered myself to the Virgin Queen
as the little victim of her Heavenly Loveliness
and her Divine and Human Love.

Mary's Will

I have not a very strong body,
I have not a lion's heart,
I have not the brain of Aquinas,
nor Michelangelo's art.

I am not another Joseph,
the handsomest man among men,
I am not the John who stood by thee
when Jesus His vict'ry did win.

I am not your troubadour, Bernard,
your honey-tongued doctor, Marie.
I'll ne'er be a classical figure

of Christian history.

But, O my dear sweet Lady Mary,
I've got me a name of steel!
And it means that I love you forever
for the Church's eternal weal.

For thy name is Mary the Virgin,
who stood upon Calvary Hill.
And my name? Thou knowest, Maria,
my name is the name of thy Will.

Mary and John the Baptist

At the sound of your greeting my heart leapt for joy
in the womb of my Mother fair.
And you are my Mother, and I am your boy –
my true Mother, always there.

Yet would I love you, dear Mary all mine,
not only as your little boy,
but even as lover his Bride fair and fine –
somehow I'd quest for such joy.

But only in Joseph could such a thing be,
and only in Jesus the King.
I say of them both and most fittingly,
"He must increase," though it sting.

But I'm fond and foolish, and quickly I see
that it's best that it be this way,
and deep in my heart I kneel before thee,
and "I must decrease," I say.

I must decrease till there's none of me left,
but only my Lady Thee,

only you, Mary, of all pride bereft,
my Lady Humility.

The Dark Knight of the Virgin

I am the dark knight of the Virgin,
I fight many battles for her.
I'm sinful and weak,
fight with tongue in my cheek –
but, oh, how I do love the Virgin!

I'm called the dark knight of the Virgin
because, though I fight in her cause,
I'm still just a sinner –
'tis she makes me winner.
Yes, oh, how I do love the Virgin!

I am the dark knight of the Virgin,
the Lady of Guadalupe.
I'll live for her story
and die for her glory –
forever knight of the Dark Virgin.

Prayer

Lord Jesus Christ, let me be an instrument of Your
Mother's.
Where she is neither known nor loved
let me make her both known and loved supremely
for Your own honor and glory.
Amen.

Prayer

Mary, Hidden Lady,
hiding in my heart,
my Queen,
Mother of God and our Mother,
I want to consecrate my heart to you once again.
I want to give myself to you,
all that I am, all that I ever will be.
After all my infidelities I come to you once again
to begin anew to love you.
I want to love you, Mary, to *begin* to love you.
Have I ever really loved you?
Have I loved you as Joseph or Bernard loved you?
Mary, I have never really been anything but selfish.
I have loved you for the joy of it.
I have loved you for your favors.
I have loved you for the gifts you give.
I have loved you for my own happiness.
Now, dear Lady, my dearest Mary, let me begin to give you
happiness and pleasure.
Let me love you in truth, in faith.
O Hidden Lady, I believe in you,
even when you hide from me.
You hide from my superficial devotion.
You hide from my phoney protestations.
You hide until I seek you with my whole heart,
and all the truth and power of my soul.
You hide from me rightly, most beautiful Mary,
for I am a false and shallow person, lazy,
who seek only gratification,
even in my love for you.

And that is the purest truth.
O Mary, now, at this late date,
help me to begin to love you in truth, in faith, in purity,
and in perfect and utter fidelity.
Most beautiful Mary, I beg it in the name of Jesus.
Lead me to Him.
Teach me His divine love,
that with you and Him
I may walk honestly and uprightly,
always,
toward the Father of Heaven
in the power of the Holy Spirit.
Amen.

His Mother

I stood there on the Mountain they call Calvary
and saw the soldier open up His side,
and when there came out blood and water only,
I did not waver – no, I simply died.

Lady of the Lake

Lady of peace and prayer,
softly dispelling my care,
Lady of calm and quiet,
Keeping me here close by it.

Mirror of love and purity,
making these waters surety
for my poor heart

by your sweet art.

Lady of eventide,
and of the water wide,
Lady of sunset gold,
in August before the cold.

Maid of the evening air,
Maid teaching me your prayer,
"Ave, Maria, the Lord is with you,"
telling me He's with me too.

Lady of my poor eyes,
looking on the hill's rise,
loving the green of the pines,
enjoying your lightest wines.

Lady of beauty rare,
Lady of peace and prayer,
Lady of lake and land,
Mary, ... hold me by the hand.

Being With You

O Mary, I sit here in your presence, in peace.
I am still and quiet.
Thoughts come –
and with them the amazing realization that you love me.
O Most Wonderful Lady!
It seems incredible that you should love me.
God has created a good thing in me,
but I have so often failed to live up to His gift.
You did not fail, Mary – ever.
I have done despicable things, time after time.

And yet you still see in me the image of God, and love me.
Somehow you even love me for my very own self,
me who often feel so very unlovable.
O Mary, truly you are magnificent!
And all I can do is humble myself before you.
My Lady! My Mother!
Amen.

Joy

Some time back I went up to my cell
to the picture of Holy Mary of Guadalupe
that I keep there over my bed
to consult her, as I am accustomed, about what to do next.
It seemed to me that she said to me very playfully,
"You just go down to the church and suffer a little bit."
So I went down to the church obediently.
As soon as I walked in,
Father Joachim walked up to me with a couple of pictures of Mary in his hand
and said, "There was a man here a while ago who left these for you."
It seemed to me that my Lady just smiled.
Well, today I was up in my cell again.
I was kissing the floor before Mary's picture
and hoping for some direction about what to do next.
It seemed to me that she said,
"Go on down to the church. But this time you really will have to suffer. But go with my blessing."
So I came on down here to the church, where I am now.
I am kneeling before the Blessed Sacrament, writing this.

I am not suffering, at least not too much,
though it is true that I always carry around in my heart that
"little bundle of the sufferings of Jesus"
that St. Bernard said we should.
But nothing is happening.
I will get up and walk,
and see what the Blessed Mother has in store for me.
I stop at the open Bible in the side aisle.
I read the Gospel of St. Luke about Zacheus.
Zacheus was a small man.
He was physically small.
I am spiritually small.
I am little and petty.
I do things that are mean and small.
I am not magnanimous.
But Jesus came and stayed in Zacheus' house,
and Zacheus welcomed him joyfully.
That's always the way it is.
When Jesus comes to stay in the little house of our soul,
no matter how pitiful and poor and disgusting a specimen
of the human race we may be,
everything is transformed into joy.
O my Lady Mary, this is your little gift of joy to me,
the gift of Jesus.
How often I go to Scripture and find nothing there.
Today there is this precious little pearl of joy.
O Mary, my exquisite Pearl, my Lady, my Joy,
Causa Nostrae Laetitiae,
thank you.
Amen.

Love

I knelt and kissed Our Lady's foot,
kissed it not once but twice.
As Mary smiled upon me there,
the Spirit said, "That's nice."

St Joseph's Day, 1989

I'm at the end of my rope again,
and I just don't know what to do.
So I come once more to the House of God,
and I sit here all bleak and blue.

And I wonder what the Lord's gonna do
to bail me out this time.
And I even wonder how He can help me
simply to finish this rhyme.

It's St. Joseph's Day, and the sun is out,
but it's raining inside my heart –
and all I can do is write it down,
for that's the extent of my art.

O great St. Joseph, can you do the job?
Can you pull me out of this gloom?
Can you make the sun shine within my heart?
Open windows into its room?

I know you can, St. Joseph dear,
I know you can do anything.
You have only to ask the Blessed Mother
to speak to Jesus the King.

And the King will grant whatever you ask,

even for a wretch like me.
Ask Him, St. Joseph, for what is best
in the light of Eternity.

I suppose what I need is more living faith
to see all the beauty around me,
a strong, living faith in the God of Love,
who makes all His angels surround me.

Then get me this faith, St. Joseph dear,
and fill it all full with love,
and I shall be glad in the sunshine of God,
which comes down to me from above.

Love

I gave my heart to the Virgin Mary –
she gave me her own.
Now I walk with the Mother of God –
I'll never walk alone.

Love

I was six years old.
My mother said to me,
"I don't care if the whole world is playing outside!
It's raining, and you may not!"
I was fifty-one years old.
Mary said to me,
"I don't care if the whole world is leaving the Church,
or the priesthood,
or the religious life,

or the Monastery!
It's infidelity, and you may not!"

O Mary

If I were a blade of grass,
and you were a beautiful dewdrop,
how lovingly I'd support you!
How lovingly I'd support you!

Grace

One thing I want to do when I go to Heaven
is to learn to ice skate.
I'm sure I'll be able to do it extremely well.
I'll ask Mary to skate with me.
I'll take her hand and put my arm around her
and hold her firmly but ever so gently,
as a man holds the woman he loves.
We will glide across the ice together,
our movements perfectly synchronized in exquisite grace.
She will look up into my eyes and smile at me,
and it will be Heaven.
Of course, everyone in Heaven will want to skate with
Mary.
I'll have to wait my turn.
But even if I have to wait forever,
Mary,
I'll wait.

Yellow Ribbons

O Mary, I have been unfaithful,
many times,
and I am ashamed.
About all I can claim is a kind of "material" fidelity.
That is, I have somehow managed to persevere so far in celibacy.
I am a miserable, pitiful thing.
And yet the Holy Spirit says to me,
"Though your sins be as scarlet, they shall become white as snow."
Mine certainly are "as scarlet."
O Mary, this is truly a word of mercy.
But can I really hope for such a thing?
O Mother of God, I long for this.
I turn to you, and I think of the song –
"Tie a yellow ribbon 'round the old oak tree...."
O Mary, I have betrayed,
I have betrayed Jesus, your Son, by my infidelities.
I have soiled my heart.
I have failed through weakness, over and over again.
I have given way to the world.
I have conformed.
O Mary, do you still want me?
And the wondrous answer comes:
A million yellow ribbons!
Amen.

An Army of Galahads

Joseph was Mary's Galahad,
and I would like to be too.
I make to you a prayer, my Lady,
with this end in view.

O Mary! Make me a Galahad!
With a heart that' s pure and true!
Hold my heart in your lovely hands –
Wound it! Wound it anew!

Make it pure, Mary, make it true,
and give me the strength of ten.
Give me the strength of *ten thousand*,
Mary, make me a leader of men!

Give me a heart that's pure and true,
make me a Galahad,
then multiply me a millionfold
to make your own heart glad.

An army of Galahads, Marie,
to defend your purity,
to love you and serve you and die for you
and give you the victory.

The battle is waging fierce and hot,
and the dragon seems to gain,
but with faith in you we shall not fail,
for we shall not heed any pain.

We will fight, Dear Lady, as Galahads,
we will fight to win a smile.
We will die for love and purity.

You will keep our hearts from guile.

You will keep them pure and true, O Mary,
  Mother and Queen of God.
Advance! God wills it! Mary does!
Our Lady has given her nod!

Mother of Mercy

Mary, Mother of Mercy,
have mercy on me.
For, oh, sweet Lady,
I'm in love with thee!

The Queen of Galilee

She would walk to the well,
she would walk to the market,
  making happy the birds and the flowers.
She would hum a sweet tune,
she would smile a sweet smile,
  and the children attend her for hours.

To know her was bliss,
to be with her was heaven,
  to speak with her joy beyond measure.
To hear her kind words
and meet her kind glance
  was nothing but wondrous pure pleasure.

She was just a young girl
with a small Baby Boy
  and a husband who worked long and hard.

Yet she spread joy around her
as she went through her tasks
    like a fragrance of perfume or nard.

She would play with her Baby
and get Him to smile,
    as He looked wond'ring into her eyes.
She would smile on her husband
whose heart would dilate
    as a man's love with woman's love vies.

But it always was she who
would win at this game,
    and for Joseph to lose was pure joy –
for he knew that the Baby God
she fondled so
    had made every man to her but a boy.

Yes, this girl was Mother
and Queen of us all –
    pretty Queen of the whole world was she.
But to all who lived 'round,
to whom the future lay hid,
    she was yet but Queen of All Galilee.

Pearl of the Universe

The woman sat enthroned beyond the stars,
and worlds obeyed her ev'ry least command.
The galaxies all served her as they whirled.
On earth praise rose to her from ev'ry land.

The Woman's name was Mary, Virgin Queen
of all that is, 'neath God's own reign supreme.
The spiral nebulae obeyed her will.
She blessed the sun, the moon, their ev'ry beam.

The earth too lovingly the Woman blessed,
each human heart she lovingly caressed,
she who in brilliant sunlight hues was dressed
and bounteous Christ her Lord and God confessed.

What shall we say of such great charity,
and *love*, that bounds knew none, infinity
transcending with the warmth of Mother's Heart,
outdoing all creation with its art?

Well, this great Lady one day had a need.
She sought to find a knight upon white steed.
But where to look in this the new space age,
when knights had vanished to the past's umbrage?

She sought throughout the whole vast universe,
throughout the cosmos, space and time she scanned,
to find a knight, a solitary knight,
who by her task would not be all unmanned.

She sought the earth, the heavens too she sought,
and found at last a little puny man
with will of steel who'd many a battle fought,

though small of stature, and she said, "He can!"

And he became the Woman's little knight.
Her little Will she called him from the height
of her great majesty and glory bright,
and into his soul poured all mystic light.

She strengthened him with virtue for the fight,
endowed him with all prowess and all might
to venture forth for her into the night,
beyond all black holes to defend the right.

He rode the steed she gave him, brilliant white,
into the deep, dark citadels of night
and conquered all the enemies of light
for her sake whose great love lent him the might.

He rode and rode through worlds of darkness black
for love of her black hair, and fell in love
with this his task that peril none did lack
for only thought that she waited above.

He conquered ev'ry darkness in this role,
transformed it into brilliant beauty whole,
and rode on till at last he reached anew
the daylight heavens sparkling clear and blue.

For he had ridden for a Lady Dear,
in pow'r of love for her who ruled his heart,
preserved his soul and kept him without fear
by all the heav'nly power of Woman's art.

He rode on till he came unto her throne,
dismounted, knelt before his Lady own.
And what reward did she keep in her Heart

for him who honestly had done his part?

She rose from her great throne of majesty,
descended steps of stars to where he knelt.
She bade him rise and clasped him to her Heart,
and bliss within him, such great bliss he felt

that all his being melted into hers.
He knew such love as man has never known.
The kiss she printed on his heart remains,
though that heart seemed to him forever flown

to Paradise on wings of joy and peace,
where – and this was the miracle she wrought –
his own small stature she made to increase,
till lacked he nothing of the height he ought.

Pure Mary

Purer than purity, you,
fairer than fairness are you,
prettier than the stars
shining in the blue.

Lovelier than love are you,
more blessed blessedness too,
greater than greatness,
gentler than the dew.

Wondrous as wonder are you,
better than goodness by two,
sweeter than sweetness,
oh, perfumed Flower, you!

The Lily

A lily is a sweet and lovely sight.
Its fragrance is a pure and chaste delight.
It sanctifies the air
with its perfume and the rare
    sweetness of a sweet and fragrant summer night.

But I'd like to speak to you of one I know
who is more a Lily, brighter than the snow,
than the fairest of that kind.
Though her beauty drive me blind,
    yes, I'd like to speak to you of one I know.

I am thinking of a certain Flower sweet,
a living Lily whom in prayer I daily greet.
Yes, this Lily is a Lady
growing in a garden shady,
    in a garden fenced in by my own heartbeat.

For my heart's a garden where my Lily grows,
and her name I think now everybody knows.
She's the Virgin Mary blessed,
both by Heaven and earth confesséd
    as the brightest Lily, brighter than the snows.

Flow'ry language has somewhat gone out of style.
But I'd like to bring it back as if by trial,
to see whether just maybe
it might once again the day be
    to praise Woman as the Flower without guile.

Don't you think that maybe this is still the truth?
Don't you think that from Naomi and from Ruth,
through Elizabeth and Ann,

somehow perhaps we can
    use a little flow'ry language with all truth?

For it somehow has to be that every girl
is a precious, precious, precious, precious pearl.
Nay, she's more than this, she's flower,
gracing sweetest summer bower
    she's the Lily Mary of th' entrancing curl.

And, my friend, if you should think it necessary
from this my sound opinion yours to vary,
then know this, thou wise and wary,
that it's very, very, very
more than that, complete – contrary
    to the utter Truth that lives within my Mary.

For my Mary lives within each flower fair,
and I'll die for this Truth surely as the air
into my lungs doth flow
as hither and yon I go
    slaying dragons for my Lily everywhere.

Lily of the Valley

O Lady, I'm not worthy,
of the Lily I can't speak –
I will write poems of the Mystic Rose
and kiss her on the cheek.

I will kiss you with "Hail Mary's,"
but since you're the Lily too,
will you count it as Lily poem,
O my Lady all in blue?

For the lilies of the field,
who neither spin nor sow nor reap,
have not your humility,
O Lily of the Valley deep.

The Theology of the Castle

Once in a castle white and grand
there lived a Maiden fair.
She was the Fairest in all the land,
loved by the very air.

The castle was her home, you see,
where lived she all her days,
most perfect in her purity,
holy in all her ways.

She lived there safe from all the taint
of a wily, wicked world.
She prayed and worked nor e'er did faint,
a Flower God-empearled.

Now one day there raised up its head
against the castle grand
the dragon of th' eternal dead
and 'gan to stalk the land.

It came unto the castle near
and breathed forth fiery flames
against th' impregnable fortress dear
as 'gainst all virtuous dames.

The Virgin Lady deep within
that glorious castle strong,

a perfect Maid and free from sin,
prayed this melodious song –

"My soul doth magnify the Lord,
my spirit joys in Him,
for He alone is God adored,
my Virtue and my Vim."

And at these words a Mighty Champ
upon the field was seen
a-riding toward the castle's ramp
and at the beast obscene.

He rode a white horse strong and fleet,
and on His thigh was writ,
The King of Kings and Lord Unbeat."
The dragon hard He hit.

The beast cried out in agony,
and it groveled in the dust,
and the Knight, dropped of His great horse free,
dispatched it with one thrust.

The Sword He used was His Holy Name,
the Word of God Most High,
and the powers of hell's deep black ill-fame
ne'er again came the castle nigh.

And the Knight rode in and took the Maid
into His chaste embrace.
Christ Jesus' glory ne'er shall fade,
nor Mary's fullness of grace.

Mary's Heel

O my lovely Lady Mary,
make me a jewel in your crown!
O my Mistress Virgin Mary,
make me a thread in your gown!

O my sweetest Mother Mary,
make me a ring on your finger!
O my Queen and Sister Mary,
ever with you to linger.

O my Beautiful One, my Mary,
make me the sole of your slipper!
O mine Empress, O my Mary,
yes, the heel of your slipper!

The Ballad of the Mystic Rose

O my friends, let me now tell you
of a Flower that once bloomed
in a mystic land across the sea –
as death and destruction loomed.

Oh, this Flower was the rare one,
oh, how fair she was to see!
Yes, this Flower was prepared of God
from all Eternity.

She diffused a perfume o'er her land,
and that perfume the winds
diffused throughout the cosmos
and unto creation's ends.

A delicate bloom, a Rose she was,

that grew in peace and free,
that grew for love and piety
of the Blessed Trinity.

She was holy, she was lovely,
she was wholly beautiful,
she the Flower God had chosen
who would be most dutiful.

She would give His Heart eternal joy
and serve Him perfectly.
She would give Him to the world a Boy
and keep her virginity.

She would watch Him grow and love Him
as to manhood He advanced.
She would marvel at His wisdom,
at His strength she'd stand entranced.

She watched o'er Him as a Mother,
as a Mother blest and true.
But He lived a life beyond her –
that was why she dressed in blue.

Then she saw the world reject Him,
and then witnessed all the pain
that th' approaching end brought with it,
and she struggled might and main

to know what she could contribute
to the solacing of Him
who for all the world's salvation
gave up all His strength and vim.

Then she saw them come to get Him,

and they carried Him away,
and she followed weeping tears that hurt,
tears that she could not stay –

till they crucified Him on a Cross
so very shamefully,
nailing Him there and counting Him
good riddance, themselves free.

But the lance they drove into His Heart,
it entered her Heart too,
and it changed her robe to brilliant red
that robe that had been blue.

Yes, it was connaturality,
or call it sympathy,
that the Mother Rose turned all blood red
when the Son died on the Tree.

My Star

Lovely and bright,
high in the evening sky,
above the black lace of the branching trees
and the rose of the setting sun.
Oh, it's more than beauty!
    It's love!
Quae est ista?
"Beautiful as the moon,"
hiding playfully behind the clouds.
"The unreachable star"?
In a way, yes, Mary,
Star so far in magnitude from me.

Yet I'd rather be your failure
than anyone else's success!
So I will go on reaching out to you anyway,
through and beyond death.
For chivalry will never die, Lady,
as long as you live.
Truly, the new knighthood is for fools
who dare to hope
for the Gift of Mary.

Wisdom

O Blessed and Glorious Ever Virgin Mary,
    I have sought after you from the days of my youth.
I sought to take you for my Bride,
and was enamored of your beauty,
for long ago you had stolen my heart.
But I hesitated,
till one day the answer came,
"...do not be afraid to take Mary to yourself...
SHE WILL EMBRACE YOU LIKE A YOUNG BRIDE."
And now I realize
how wise I was to hope.
Amen.

The Gift of Mary

I really only have one gift,
and that is the gift of Mary –
the gift that Jesus gave me when He said,
"Son, there is your Mother...
Woman, there is your son."
But this one gift is for me the gift of all things,
for everything I need
is the gift of Mary,
a gift to me from you, Lady –
fidelity
purity,
the Holy Spirit –
Jesus.

My Prayer

O my Lady, Holy Mary,
make me a channel of God's grace.
Where there is doubt and confusion,
let me bring His certainty and peace.
Where there is weakness and fear,
let me bring His strength and confidence.
Where there is anguish and distress,
use me to bring the surrender of living faith and love.
Where there is any kind of suffering or hopelessness or
sense of meaninglessness,
grant that I may bring the fullness and wholeness
of the wonderful Holy Spirit,
our God and your Spouse.
Amen.

Afterwords

Once Upon A Time

St. Joseph, Patron of
True Devotion to Mary

Once Upon A Time

There lived a knight. He was called The Knight of the Burning Cheeks. For every time he saved a damsel in distress from a dragon he would blush violently crimson from ear to ear at her expressions of gratitude.

Now it happened one day that the great Virgin Mary appeared to this humble knight to make of him a request. She told him how her wonderful Kingdom of Beautiful Love was in dire danger from a certain malevolent foe, called the Prince of Dragons. She requested the Knight of the Burning Cheeks to search out this enemy and crush him – for her sake.

Now the Knight of the Burning Cheeks had, it goes without saying, fallen to his knees at the first glimpse of the Beautiful Vision. When he heard the challenge offered him by so lovely and noble a Lady, his heart leapt burning within him, and he yearned to be in action, in the service of the Queen of Queens.

The Virgin gave her knight information as to how to find this enemy in his own lair, where he must be fought to be conquered completely and utterly, and then with a confident and loving smile vanished, leaving a delicious perfume in the air as a token of her love and gratitude to her chosen warrior.

The knight set out immediately, praying as he rode. He rode forty days and forty nights on his splendid charger, without sleeping or eating – until finally he came to a dark woods. It was the darkest woods he had ever seen, impenetrably dark – Black! Yet here he had been assured by the incomparable Virgin he would encounter the deadly foe. He entered The Black Forest.

He rode slowly, in total darkness. He heard not a sound. Not a breath of air stirred. In fact, it seemed to him, almost, that there *was* no air.

He rode on. He rode on and on and on. He prayed for keenness, for penetration, for awareness. He prayed to the Virgin: Ave, Maria! Ave, Maria! Ave, Mari-*a*!

The attack had come! On the third syllable of the Holy Name! Instantly the knight was all and total alertness! He felt his horse sink to the earth beneath him without a sound. The Dragon, faster than a rattlesnake, had struck the neck of the noble charger, and immediately – though the knight knew it not – the neck was nothing but a mass of blood. The horse was dead at the one strike.

The knight now found himself standing on the ground, his lance useless. At once he ceased to think of it. It fell from his hand.

He drew his sword and waited. He had seen nothing.

He stood waiting, ready. Still, he saw nothing.

For hours, from his entrance into the Blackness, he

had heard not so much as the fall of a leaf or the movement of a bird's wing. In a flash, he knew the name of the Blackness: The Realm of the Dragon! He had ridden into ... <u>HELL</u>! – for a heavenly <u>Cause</u>! Now, if he would proceed further, he must proceed on foot. He must walk. He must march.

He stepped forward. He realized that a second lightning attack would be the end of him. He prayed "Jesu! Maria! Joseph! ... Joanne Baptista!"

He was walking, very, very slowly, his eyes trying to the utmost to pierce the impenetrable Blackness.

Now the Dragon had the burning eyes of a devil. He could see in the Blackness of his domains, see acutely. Yet in this very fact of the burning eyes lay the knight's one chance. The eyes could be seen in the total darkness – the eyes of an intellectual reptile .... The knight had not seen them when his horse was attacked and destroyed, for the cunning of the Dragon had kept them beneath the body of the horse.

Still, the knight did not know this, or he would have feared only an attack from behind.

Realizing that his eyes would betray him in the darkness, the Dragon had fled immediately on accomplishing his initial purpose.

Need we say that the Prince of Dragons was the greatest of cowards and would only attack the person of a knight from behind? It is the truth.

The knight moved slowly, ever so slowly, cautiously,

but withal resolutely onward. He was on mission, the supreme mission of his life. He must not fail.

He would not fail.

He walked on.

After about a hour, he suddenly perceived a faint odor.

Now the Dragon, you must know, had a terrible stench. The knight may have remarked something of it at the death of his horse, but the attack had been of such lightning speed, that it had not been significant. Now, though, the Dragon proceeded – even from behind – slowly and cautiously.

This was his undoing.

The malodorous smell grew in the knight's nostrils. It nearly made him sick. Yet as it grew worse, he felt joy grow in his heart, for he knew the foe was near.

The knight strained every nerve, every fiber of his being, to sense where the horrible stench was coming from. Suddenly he realized.

From behind!

He whirled, and met the blazing, cowardly eyes of the Dragon. To plunge his faithful sword into the heart beneath them, driving it home with all the whole might of a strong man, was the work of a split second.

Instantaneously, an incredible bellow of agony filled the Black Forest whose echoes resounded deafeningly through the dark realm for minutes.

Then there was silence again.

The knight knew that his thrust had been totally effective, when he saw the evil light slowly fade from the eyes of the diabolical beast.

In the utter and absolute darkness, he withdrew his wondrous sword from the dull, heavy body of his – and the Virgin's – conquered foe.

He turned around and walked – forward, continuing in the same direction he had so far come.

He walked for about a half hour. Then suddenly he saw a faint light. It was good light. It was the end of the Dragon's domains.

The knight soon found himself out of the terrible woods. After some walking he began to notice familiar landmarks and shortly made his way back to his residence.

He ate heartily that evening and slept well that night.

At dawn the Virgin Mary appeared to him once again. She greeted him with the words, "Well done, good and faithful servant."

He knelt before her in joyful Love.

She went on in accents of tenderest devotion and womanly Love. "Because you have succeeded, the Black Forest will disappear. Little by little the darkness will give way to the good light. Within a million years, the wondrous power of the good light of God will completely eliminate the evil darkness of that woods. The woods will gradually, little by little, be reborn. And the day will come when the black darkness will have disappeared utterly and absolutely, totally and completely, from the memories of every people. Rejoice, My Knight. There is joy among my angels."

Then the Queen of Beautiful Love reached down and gracefully withdrew the knight's sword from its scabbard. Extending it, she touched it to his heart.

As she held it there she pronounced these words: "Knight of the Burning Cheeks you shall be called no longer. I give you a new name for all eternity. Henceforth, you shall be known as –

'The Knight of the Virgin Mary.'

"As a token of my gratitude, and my affection, in my Loving Mercy, I grant you The Gift of Love, seven Wounds of Love in your heart, one for each of the Seven Sorrows I suffered to co-redeem the world with and in subordination to Our Lord and God, Jesus Christ, my Son."

Then she plunged the sword delicately into his poor ecstatically blissful heart, seven times, in seven different places, while at each plunge the knight died a thousand joyful deaths of Love, Love, Love!

She replaced the sword in the knight's scabbard. He never withdrew it again. Perhaps he never would have been able to. In any case, it was not necessary.

After she had returned the sword, with a smile that seemed to render his whole heart but one great wound of

Love, she vanished. Nor was there any perfume left behind her this time. For the knight whose senses were suspended from their operations, could never have noticed any.

Needless to say, the knight spent the rest of his days in prayer, and died not long after with the lovely name of his Lady on his lips.

All that she said came true.

For century after century the darkness of the awful woods grew less and less. Toward the end of the million years there remained only a few square feet of it. And when that was gone, the black woods was no more. There was throughout the whole world only one Wood, and in every tree was found a "Tree All Beauteous," made so by the good light of Beautiful Love.

This is the story of how the Virgin, Mother and Queen of Beautiful Love triumphed for all her children.

Amen! Alleluia! Deo Gratias et Mariae!

St. Joseph
Patron of True Devotion to Mary

It seems to me that St. Joseph should be the "patron saint of evolution," because that is what his name means – development, progress, growth, "increase."

Scripture calls him a "just man." He is the silent man. Not one word of his is recorded in the Bible. He is the archtype of all strong, silent people.

Pope Leo XIII said ("Quamquam Pluries") that St. Joseph is the greatest saint in Heaven after Mary, because he was the closest to Jesus and Mary. Jesus, Mary and Joseph, the Holy Family, belong to the order of the hypostatic union, as the great theologian, Suarez, teaches. Thus St. Joseph is even more important and more necessary for us than the great Michael the Archangel or John the Baptist. The Litany of St. Joseph calls him the "terror of the demons."

St. Thomas Aquinas says that we pray to the other saints for particular things, but to St. Joseph for *everything*. St. Joseph is the Spouse of the Blessed Virgin Mary and the foster or "putative" father of Our Lord Jesus Christ, the Incarnate Word, the Divine Son of God the Father. These are his greatest and principal titles.

Because he was the head of the Holy Family, St. Joseph is the Patron of the Universal Church, which is the Family or People of God. He was a carpenter who worked long and hard to support Jesus and Mary. He taught this trade to Jesus. He is therefore also the Patron Saint of Workers and will keep every one who prays to him from hunger or need. He will help us all to find good, human work, adapted to our particular aptitudes, or at least honest work that we are able to do. Finally, he is the Patron Saint of a Happy Death, because – as Tradition says – he died in the arms of Jesus and Mary.

We pray to St. Joseph in a special way for the grace and gift of chastity. He is often represented holding a lily, for this virtue was his in an absolute degree.

Truly, if as St. Thomas Aquinas says, there is a certain "infinite" dignity to Mary, the Mother of God, there surely must be a certain "infinite" humility to St. Joseph, who served her so lovingly and who may be called the least in the Kingdom of Heaven after the humble Virgin Mary.

The great St. Teresa of Avila says in her autobiography that whoever wants to become a saint and cannot find an adequate spiritual director should take St. Joseph for his or her guide, and he or she will not stray from the right path.

> Make us go through life innocent, St. Joseph,
> and keep us safe under your protection.
> Amen.

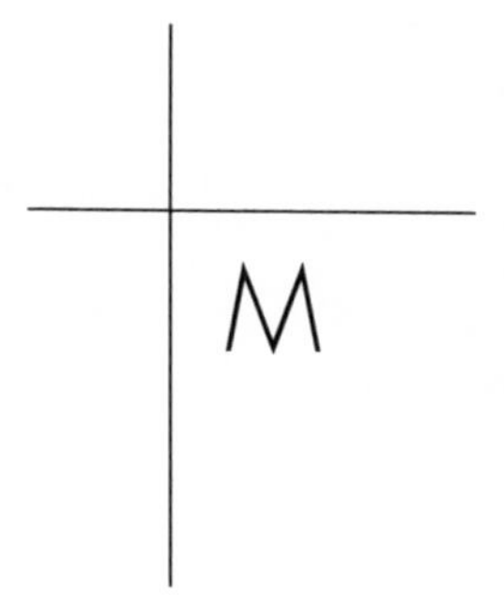
M

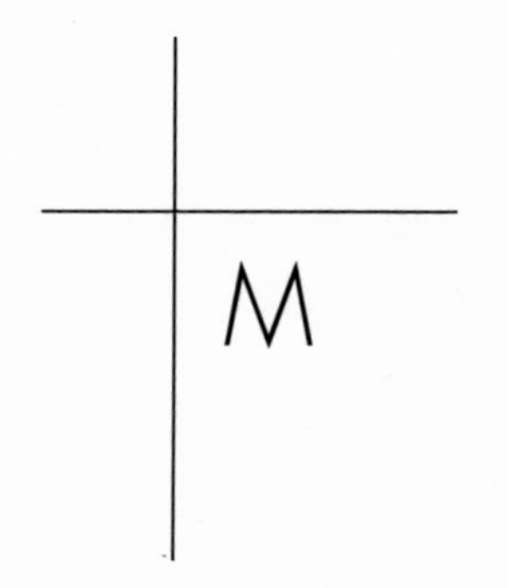